TRUTH

THE KORDELL STEWART STORY

KORDELL STEWART

WITH STEPHEN COPELAND
FOREWORD BY LEIGH STEINBERG

PRAISE FOR TRUTH

"I've had the pleasure of knowing Kordell for well over a decade. His love for life, his passion for others, and his consistency in being the man he was called to be is more than admirable. Over the years, I've witnessed him walk through the storms of life and deal with the juvenility of people, but he continues to be the nice, sincere, kind-hearted man I always knew. He does not compromise his values or harbor resentment toward others. Kordell knows his truth and lives it out."

-Deion Sanders, NFL Pro Football Hall of Famer

"Kordell Stewart was really the first dual-threat quarterback of the new era. He had an amazing gift of speed coupled with a great football IQ. Kordell was a great teammate of mine, but as good of a player and teammate as he was, he is an even better friend. Kordell, thank you for your friendship. I know you are a success in life so I expect *Truth: The Kordell Stewart Story* to be a success as well!"

-Jerome Bettis ("The Bus"), NFL Pro Football Hall of Famer

"I always enjoyed Kordell as Slash on the field, but he's just as entertaining off of the field. I had the pleasure of working with him for several years at ESPN and his energy, personality, and storytelling always stood out and kept your attention. This book is sure to do the same thing for you."

-Mike Hill, former ESPN anchor and current Fox Sports 1 host

"Kordell revered his dad like no other father-son relationship I've ever been around. It was a true joy to have observed their love towards one another, and I know this book will capture the special bond that they had. Their relationship was an encouragement to me, and I hope it will be an encouragement to you through this book."

-**Dewayne Washington, former teammate and cornerback for the Pittsburgh Steelers**

"Playing football with Kordell in Pittsburgh was great. He taught me the meaning of professionalism. His approach to the game was bar none! I will always be thankful that I got to have Stew as a teammate!"

-**Hines Ward, former teammate and wide receiver for the Pittsburgh Steelers**

"Kordell was one of the most gifted athletes to ever play quarterback in the NFL. I wonder how good he would have been if his style of play was accepted back when we played."

-**Chad Scott, former teammate and cornerback for the Pittsburgh Steelers**

"Kordell was a quiet leader with skills that he sharpened through the daily process of pursuing his social, academic, and athletic endeavors. His ability to work diligently to develop these skills always helped him gain the trust of the people that surrounded him. He was truly a blessing in many people's lives, and I know this book will help him to do the same in many more people's lives."

-**Tom Lavigne, Kordell's high school football coach**

TABLE OF CONTENTS

FOREWORD
INTRO

PART III: FATHER

FOREWORD

By Leigh Steinberg, Sports Agent

I had the extraordinary pleasure of representing Kordell Stewart throughout his professional football career and will always represent his best interests.

Sometimes our relationship was reversed. When a day became problematic or stressful, I had a ready antidote: I would pick up the phone and call Kordell. His ever-present optimism, joy and sense of humor are a tonic. He walks through the world bringing hope and healing wherever he goes. His charisma and warmth draw people to him, and the world is his friend.

He has faced loss and adversity since childhood. Losing his mother so young was traumatic. The loss of extended family members added to the grief. He responded with resilience and perspective. The door was opened to one of the closest imaginable father-son relationships with his father Robert. He has always treasured family and relationships.

After a storied college career, there were doubts in the NFL about Kordell's capacity to play the quarterback position. At one point coming into the 1995 Draft, he was the 31st-rated quarterback available. He was resolute about not switching positions and never doubted his ability. He used the scouting period to orchestrate one of the fastest ever elevations in draft status. He just missed being a first rounder and was drafted in the second by the Pittsburgh Steelers.

The whole football world was transfixed by his role as "Slash" his rookie season. He was a dynamic threat as a running quarterback, halfback and wide receiver. Football had never seen anything quite like it. He took the lemon status of a backup quarterback and, as usual, made electrifying lemonade from it. When his time to start came, he took his team to the playoffs, went to the Pro Bowl, and finished third in League MVP voting. Starting quarterbacks need the full support of their coaches so they can slowly develop their skills. Kordell never received that consistent support. But he never grew bitter or complained.

Kordell has been the epitome of a great role model. His love of God, family, and friends has never wavered. He is a committed and loving father to his son, Syre. As you read his inner feelings regarding his journey, remember this—Kordell has never stopped trying to bring happiness to those around him. Think of a ray of sunshine, and you get the essence of Kordell Stewart.

INTRO

By Kordell Stewart

Adapt. Get it done. *Slash.*

As a verb, the word "slash" exudes force and strength. It is usually used in the context of something or someone coming face-to-face with some sort of resistance—an obstacle to overcome.

Marshawn Lynch slashed through the defense.

The general slashed through the enemy's frontlines.

For me, "slash" was used as a noun because it was my nickname. Some people say Pittsburgh Steelers radio announcer Myron Cope was the first to call me "Slash." Others say it was Steelers head coach Bill Cowher. I credit both of them. They gave me this nickname back in 1995 because of my ability to play different positions. I was a quarterback-*slash*-running back-*slash*-wide receiver-*slash*-punter; I played multiple positions in my NFL career.

For the Steelers, I played all those positions because I wanted to but also because they needed me to in the wake of various injuries on offense. I was a quarterback for four years at the University of Colorado, but in Pittsburgh, I had to adapt. That meant playing different positions to help out the team so we could win—so we could get it done.

"Slash" might have been my nickname on the football field, but to me, it's more than that. It goes far beyond my role for the Pittsburgh Steelers. It's a lifestyle I try to adopt. It's a mindset I try to attain. It encompasses its standard definition as a verb but also the definition behind my nickname:

Adapt—no matter your role, no matter what position you're in, no matter the resistance you might face—and get it done.

To me, that's what "Slash" really means. And it's a mindset everyone can adopt because everyone faces trials of many kinds throughout life. Everyone, sometime or another, faces some sort of resistance.

When challenges in this life arise, I don't want to be a guy who lies around and sulks. Life is about growing as a person through both the mountaintops and the valleys. Life isn't drudgery if we refuse to believe it's drudgery. Life's challenges are actually *experiences* from which we can learn and grow.

That's what this book is about. It will take you to some extreme highs but also some extreme lows—because that's how life is. Adversity will inevitably come, but we are all challenged to adapt in the storms of life. To get it done in the midst of them. To see it through and keep on living. To press on and prevail. But the choice is yours.

———

See It Through

When you're up against a trouble,
Meet it squarely, face to face;
Lift your chin and set your shoulders,
Plant your feet and take a brace.
When it's vain to try to dodge it,
Do the best that you can do;
You may fail, but you may conquer,
See it through!

Black may be the clouds about you
And your future may seem grim,
But don't let your nerve desert you;
Keep yourself in fighting trim.
If the worst is bound to happen,
Spite of all that you can do,
Running from it will not save you,
See it through!

Even hope may seem but futile,
When with troubles you're beset,
But remember you are facing
Just what other men have met.
You may fail, but fall still fighting;
Don't give up, whate'er you do;
Eyes front, head high to the finish.
See it through!

-Edgar Albert Guest

———

PART I

BUFFALOES

1

ALWAYS SMILING

When the doctors diagnosed my mother, Florence, with cancer, they gave her three months to live. *Three months.* That's it.

What would you do if you only had three months to live? Would you start living like never before? Would you sink into sadness and despair? Would you stop living all together?

Throughout the duration of my childhood, I never really knew my mother was sick because she did not live like she had been diagnosed with cancer—which kind of speaks for itself. She did not live like she had a disease. She did not live like she had been cursed. She certainly did not venture through life as a victim, feeling sorry for herself and her circumstance. Consequently, she lived much longer than three months. Much, much longer. And I think that's primarily because of her positive attitude and joyful approach to life.

Momma was about five feet, ten inches tall. She had the body of an hourglass, with curvy, long legs. She was a beautiful woman. She had long hair and always had a smile on her face. In fact, when I think about my mom, what strikes me most is that she always seemed so joyful. She hardly wavered in her emotions. She was solid, levelheaded, and strong-willed. She was kind to everyone. Even when people made mistakes, she would give them second and third and fourth chances. That's just who she was. She was a giver and a humanitarian, and she was always there for her friends.

My father, Robert Sr., worked as a barber to pay the bills, and Momma managed the household. Mom worked at West Jefferson Hospital for a time, but eventually she made the decision to stay home to watch me, my brother Robert Jr. (who was nine years older than me), and my sister Falisha (who was six years older than me). My parents instilled values in their three children that still keep me going today. I remember the Bible studies we always used to have as a family. We would all crowd into bed with my parents, and we would take turns reading different Scriptures and talking about them. Every Sunday we drove from the West Bank of New Orleans to Nineveh Baptist Church on the East Bank. Church was an all-day ordeal—starting with Sunday School from nine to ten, service from eleven to one (sometimes two or three o'clock depending on the topic Reverend Neal was preaching on), lunch at my aunt's after service, evening service until nine or ten o'clock at night, and returning home by eleven at the latest. Church was important to my mother, which made it important to our family, which made it important to me.

The best way I can describe my family is to compare us to the 1970s sitcom *Good Times*. My sister was Thelma, my brother was J.J., and I was Sir Michael. We had values; we had traditions; and boy, did we have some good times.

Life wasn't always easy, but for us Stewarts, it was always good.

✦ ✦ ✦

My parents raised me to view the glass as half-full rather than half-empty, to enjoy living despite the storms that might pass through. This was not only something my parents preached; it was also the lifestyle they lived.

When my mother was diagnosed with cancer, I was only four or five, and my parents were expecting a fourth child. I was supposed to be a big brother. Momma gave birth to my little brother, Terrance, but a day or two after Terrance was born, he passed away due to complications in his physical development.

I cannot imagine the pain my parents must have felt. For my father, losing a son and watching his wife endure cancer had to have been agonizing. For my mother, it all had to have been overwhelming.

Yet if you entered our household on any given day, you never would have known my parents were dealing with that type of turmoil. They did not take out their stresses or hurts on their children.

It did not affect their parenting. Their pain did not overshadow their joy.

Similarly, when my parents split up a few years later, it didn't affect their parenting either. Both of them were strong-willed individuals who ended up going separate ways—yet I never sensed that they had any bitterness toward one another. Momma continued being the same, amazing mother she had always been, and Daddy continued being the same, amazing father.

✦ ✦ ✦

As Momma's battle with cancer continued, she ate raw liver or ground beef and drank a glass of wine each day—Riunite on ice—because she heard these things might help her live a little longer. She had already lasted a lot longer than three months. Who knows if those things actually helped, but her positive mental approach to her disease did keep her motivated and hopeful. The main thing I remember about Momma is that she was *always* smiling.

My mother is the reason I smile. People let life get them down way too easily. If Momma could be happy and think about others while wrestling with cancer, I can surely be happy and think outside of myself no matter what is thrown my way. Momma taught me to have a joyful heart regardless of circumstances. She taught me to be a fighter. She taught me to push through adversity.

Once, for example, when my mother was the weakest we had ever seen her, she still mustered the strength to attend my sister's high school graduation ceremony at Municipal Auditorium in New Orleans. My mother, practically on her deathbed, still supported the people she loved—and did it with a smile. Looking back at that, considering the condition she was in, I have no idea how she was able to do it. But just like she lived significantly longer than the doctor's three-month estimate, her inner strength once again allowed her to do something that most might consider impossible.

✦ ✦ ✦

All in all, Momma hung in there for five or six years after her diagnosis. She was relentless. The doctors originally gave her three months to live, and she went on to live for another half-decade.

The day Momma died, not long after Falisha's graduation, I was eleven years old. I came home from football practice after school, and Falisha was the only one in our house. I remember walking into the house and sensing something eerie.

Falisha approached me, and I could not help but notice her red, puffy eyes and the somber look on her face. She bent down and gave me a hug.

"Kordell," Falisha said softly.

I do not know why, but I knew what she was about to say.

"Mommy's gone?" I asked.

"Yep," she said. "Mommy's gone."

I started crying, not really knowing what it all meant. I knew my mother had been sick, but I was still too young to comprehend the magnitude of death and earthly separation. When you're eleven years old, the last thing you think about is someone dying in the family. All I knew was that Mom was gone, and nothing was the same.

When I saw my father that evening, he tried to comfort me. I remember him talking to me and trying to soothe me, even though he knew I couldn't understand. He encouraged me and told me everything would be okay—that Momma was smiling in heaven and that I would see her again.

I can't wait to see that smile again.

2
DADDY'S BOY

My father, the oldest boy of nine children, was much like my mother in terms of his inner strength and glass-half-full approach to life. Though he was left to raise three children on his own, he did not blink an eye. He did what he had to do to support the family and continued being the reliable father he had always been. He worked three jobs—as a painter, a carpenter, and a barber—to support the family. He was the ultimate Slash—working all those jobs and doing all those different things to provide for his family.

With both of my older siblings becoming young adults and starting their adult lives—Falisha was seventeen and Robert was twenty—they had to deal with the loss of our mom in their own ways. I was significantly younger, so I was around the house with my father much more than they were. Consequently, the death of my mother dramatically changed my relationship with my father. He became my best friend, and I became his.

My father gave me time to cry and mourn after Momma passed, but he also helped me understand that we had to keep living. It's what she would have wanted us to do. Keep living. Press on. Get it done.

Even though my mother was no longer physically with us, her spirit was still very much alive. Sometimes I would do something that was similar to things my mom had done, and Dad would say, "Boy, you just like your Momma."

I would say, "Thanks, Daddy."

All in all, my father and I needed one another. And I remember being by his side wherever he went—going to his construction sites around town, hitting golf balls with him in our backyard, and even helping him turn our garage into a barbershop. I eventually started working alongside him in the barbershop, cutting the neighborhood boys' hair and making five dollars or so per cut. I wanted to be just like Daddy, and I wanted to be next to him at all times.

My father taught me everything—from painting, to cutting hair, to catching the public transportation bus on my own and taking it across the river to see my cousins. Like my mother, Dad also taught me to smile during tough times, to think outside of myself, and to not allow trials to define me or dictate who I was as a person. I sometimes wonder what my father must have felt throughout the hardships he endured—whether it was losing Terrance, losing Momma, or raising three children on his own—but he taught me that pain inevitably comes and that what matters most is how you react to adversity.

What Dad did for me during my childhood was invaluable. At an impressionable age when I could have gone a lot of different ways with my life, Daddy made sure I stayed on the straight and narrow.

Losing a parent can lead to a lot of idle time in a child's life—there were many times when I was the only one home because my dad had to work—and that idle time can sometimes lead to a child doing things he has no business doing. This idle time can often make a child feel neglected. But I always felt loved by my father. He became my best friend, and I never wanted to let my best friend down. I only wanted to make him proud.

As a single parent today, I draw strength from the way my father parented my siblings and me. I do not know if I would be the person I am today if it wasn't for my father's intentional presence, love, and care in my upbringing. From the day my eyes opened to the day his closed, I was always by Daddy's side.

3

THE BEGINNING

My upbringing, of course, involved football.

Growing up, the kids in my neighborhood and I played a lot of football—or at least some variation of football. A lot of times, we would just play in the street with a balled up piece of paper. I remember always taking my shoes off because I felt fastest when I was barefoot.

I guess you could say that Slash, in a football sense, was born in my childhood. I wasn't just a quarterback growing up. In fact, I was rarely a quarterback. We had a whole generation of Slashes running around that neighborhood because we all wanted to play everything.

In youth football, I played nose guard and tailback. In middle school, I played cornerback, safety, receiver and quarterback. As a freshman on the junior varsity team in high school, I played cornerback and kicked field goals.

My brother Robert taught me everything I knew about the game as a youngster. He taught me to hold my hands together when catching a football, creating a diamond with my two thumbs and my two index fingers, kind of like how Jay-Z makes the "dynasty" sign. We were doing that before Jay-Z even thought about it! Maybe Jay-Z should have played receiver in the NFL.

Robert also let me play football with him and his friends. Considering most of them, like Robert, were at least nine years older than me, those scrimmages really roughed me up and forced me to be thick-skinned and tough. Though I was significantly younger, I was as fast as all of them. I realized early on that I had been gifted with speed. I would often challenge Falisha, who was a track star in high school, to footraces when I saw her.

From as young as I can remember, I was always trying to keep up with my siblings. I remember Robert sometimes taking me and my cousin Reggie to a nearby basketball court and promising us money—for a sandwich at McDonald's or a bag of potato chips at a nearby gas station—if we could steal the ball from him.

Once, he challenged me to jump off the roof of our house. I don't know why I said yes. I guess I wanted to be courageous and prove to him that I was tough enough to do whatever he wanted me to do. So I tied a blanket around my neck like Charlie Brown and jumped off the roof. It was probably a twelve-foot drop or so, and it was one of the scariest falls and hardest landings I've ever experienced. But I wanted to do it. I wanted to show my courage to him.

The reason I mention these stories is because I think every experience in my childhood helped me develop into the young man and football player that I was in high school. After losing my mother in the fifth grade, I was forced to grow up quickly. And constantly playing pickup football against kids who were nine years older than me forced me to toughen up fast.

✦ ✦ ✦

Whether my friends and I were scrimmaging with a balled-up piece of paper in the streets of Marrero or my teammates and I were playing competitive football at John Ehret High School, the game of football was an opportunity for me to escape and express myself. Having experienced a number of things in my childhood that I struggled to understand, I always enjoyed the freedom that came with playing football. I loved the nuances of the game, its challenges, the athleticism it required, the thinking it entailed, and most of all, the thrill of victory.

Growing up, football was always fun—the way football is meant to be.

✦ ✦ ✦

My opportunity to start as a quarterback at John Ehret High School came after I accidentally kicked the starting quarterback's hand during my sophomore season. Our starting quarterback's name was Ernest Calloway, nicknamed "Doobie." Because he was the quarterback, he was also the holder on our field goal unit. I was our team's field goal kicker.

Our coaches always told Doobie to hold the football with his left hand during field goals since his right hand was his throwing hand. One day in practice, however, he held the football with his right hand, and my shinbone crunched into his hand when I was attempting a field goal. Down went Doobie.

I got to start the next two or three weeks. As my career progressed through college and into the NFL, Doobie would always joke, "I know you kicked my hand on purpose, man."

Doobie went on to do pretty well himself as a wide receiver and a kick/punt returner at Purdue University, but Doobie says I got my claim to fame because I kicked his hand.

My world seemed to open up while playing quarterback for John Ehret High School. I simply tried to apply the principles my father had always taught me—hard work, discipline, and dedication—to the game of football. It wasn't difficult to apply these things because I loved the game and because Daddy had ingrained those principles in me.

Daddy once told Miss Dinah, who I consider my stepmom though they never married, "If my boy keeps doing what he's doing, he's going to play in the pros!"

"Don't put that pressure on him!" she said. "How do you know what he's going to do?"

"I don't know," he said, "but that boy is working his butt off."

When I was an upperclassman at John Ehre, recruiters around the country began taking note of my quarterbacking performances. My senior year, I was named New Orleans Offensive Player of the Year and earned a spot on the All-State team. I was amazed to find myself being sought after by schools like Syracuse, South Carolina, Arkansas, Notre Dame, LSU, Minnesota, Oklahoma, Nebraska, Florida State, Michigan, UCLA, and USC.

I couldn't believe it. I was just a kid—a senior at John Ehret High School—still cutting pictures of NFL players out of *Sports Illustrated* and pasting them on the wall in my bedroom. Yet here I was, one year away from potentially playing alongside some of the college superstars I loved to watch on television every Saturday.

Late in the recruiting process, another school began recruiting me: the University of Colorado Buffaloes under Coach Bill McCartney, one of the top football programs in the country.

Their pursuit of me changed my football career forever.

✦ ✦ ✦

My senior year of high school, I remember watching the University of Colorado play the University of Tennessee on television in the Pigskin Classic—the first game of what would become Colorado's national championship season.

I remember watching Tennessee wide receiver Carl Pickens (who went on to play in Cincinnati with quarterback Jeff Blake) and Colorado wide receiver Mike Pritchard (who went on to be selected by the Atlanta Falcons thirteenth overall in the 1991 NFL Draft). Darian Hagan was Colorado's quarterback, and as I watched him lead the offense down the field, I thought about how I was watching two of the best teams in the country and how both of them were recruiting me. *Me.*

I—the same kid who jumped off of a rooftop because his brother told him to, who loved trying to outrun his sister in sprint races, who played football simply because he loved to play football—was being recruited by two of the top college football programs in the country at the time.

My two favorite teams to watch that season were Colorado and Notre Dame—Colorado because they were my favorite team recruiting me and Notre Dame because they had my favorite quarterback, Tony Rice. Fittingly, the two teams faced each other in the Orange Bowl. The Buffaloes beat the Irish 10–9 and were awarded the *Associated Press* national championship.

I couldn't help but wonder: Would that be me one day?

✦ ✦ ✦

The first Colorado football coach to make a personal visit to Marrero was the Buffaloes' linebackers coach Bob Simmons. Coach Simmons made it very clear to me that the coaching staff wanted me to sign with them. He also mentioned that, in an era where black, mobile quarterbacks were a rarity, this style of quarterbacking was quite common in Colorado's recent history.

In 1990, for example, my senior season at John Ehret, the Buffaloes had won the national championship under the direction of Darian Hagan, who epitomized this style of quarterbacking. An African-American quarterback from California, Hagan had burst onto the college football scene the year before, accumulating more than one thousand yards passing and one thousand yards rushing in the same season, flourishing in Gary Barnett's "I-Bone" offense under Coach McCartney.

When Hagan got hurt during the1990 national championship season, another African-American quarterback named Charles Johnson backed him up. And the third-string quarterback was another African-American named Vance Joseph.

Hagan. Johnson. Joseph. All black quarterbacks. I found this very interesting, revealing, and telling. Colorado was not afraid to go against the grain and do something that was somewhat against the norm at the time.

As I thought about some of the other schools that were recruiting me, I couldn't help but wonder: Would I be given the opportunity at quarterback? Would I be accepted in an era in which my quarterbacking style wasn't very accepted? Would I be forced to play a different position?

Not only was Colorado the best football program pursuing me, but I also felt like it presented the most promise for me as a quarterback. I had visited Arkansas first, Oklahoma second, and Nebraska third, but by the time I started planning my visit to Colorado, I had the feeling I was about to experience something special.

4

CALL OF THE ROCKIES

I had never seen snow before my flight to the University of Colorado for my recruiting visit. I remember looking out of the plane window and seeing the Rocky Mountains blanketed with the white stuff. It was beautiful. For a Southern boy born and raised on the outskirts of New Orleans, it was shocking to see the drastic elevation of the Rockies—especially when contrasted with the Louisiana swampland I know so well.

Les Steckel, the quarterbacks coach, and Rick George, one of the recruiters (who is now the athletic director at Colorado), picked me up from the airport in Denver. When I arrived on campus, it was as if I had already committed to Colorado in my mind. The air was crystal clear—fresh, all natural—and I could smell the pines. I was in awe! When I saw students walking through campus, wearing their coats and carrying their backpacks, I kept envisioning myself being one of them. I kept thinking, "This place is unbelievable; this is the best lifestyle there is." I felt like the supernatural hit me in the face.

Most importantly, I would find out that weekend that the program—the players and the coaches—felt like family. Coach McCartney represented the values my family stood for. He was a family man and a man of great faith. He was genuine. It was easy to see he was all about developing young men. With all the dirty things you hear about college recruiting, it was refreshing to see that Coach McCartney did things the right way.

The player who hosted me on my visit to Boulder was a fellow quarterback named Vance Joseph. Vance was actually one of my archrivals in high school; he had attended Archbishop Shaw, located a mile from my school. His father and my father had once worked together at a sandblasting plant in Avondale Shipyard, and they were extremely close, so we were all sort of family.

When I saw Vance Joseph—my rival, neighbor, and friend—making it at Buffalo, I said to myself, "Shoot, if Vance can do it, then I can do it, too." It's not my fault they recruited two of the best quarterbacks in the state of Louisiana in back-to-back years!

Before I flew home to Louisiana, I remember walking into Coach McCartney's office at Folsom Field. Behind his desk was a big, bay-style window, and I could see a snow-capped mountain in the distance. He was sitting there at his desk, with his chair angled toward me, and as I sat there, I could not help but think about how inspired I felt by who he was and what he represented. On top of that, he had also just won a national championship. Again, I was in awe.

"So what do you think?" Coach McCartney asked me.

"Coach," I said, taking a deep breath and looking out the window once more, "wow."

He smiled.

"Coach, I have a question," I said.

"Yes?" he responded.

"Can you give me some time?"

As blown away as I was by my visit and as badly as I wanted to tell him I had decided I wanted to attend school at the University of Colorado, I also wanted to be sure I was making the right decision and not committing to something out of emotion.

"This is what we're going to do," he said, leaning forward and rubbing his hands together like he had a recipe or something. "I'm going to give you forty-eight hours to make a decision. I don't want to rush you. We're just going to give you time, and we're not going to make any moves at quarterback until we hear back from you."

"Thanks, Coach," I said. "This place is beautiful, Coach."

"I think this is going to be a great fit for you because we are going in a different direction," he said, his voice fluctuating in his excitement about the future. "With you, we could do a lot of good things."

He paused and crossed his legs.

"What I want to say," he continued, "is that we want you here. We'll give you some time. Don't worry, go talk to your dad; I know how much he means to you. We understand."

"Thanks, Coach," I said.

He then leaned over, intently looked at me, and said, "We want you here at Colorado!" and knocked his fist emphatically on his desk.

It was surreal for me, as a kid, to think about how the reigning national champions wanted me to play for them so badly. When I left campus that day to head to the airport, I felt like I might cry because I didn't want to leave that perfect place.

I fell asleep on the plane ride home and had a dream about mountains.

✦ ✦ ✦

When my plane landed in New Orleans, I went to baggage claim, and for whatever reason, I knew I was ready to commit to the University of Colorado to play for Coach Bill McCartney. I dialed 1-800-GOBUFFS there in baggage claim, even before my father had arrived to pick me up from the airport. The operator connected me to Coach McCartney, and I told him, "Coach, I'm ready to commit to Colorado."

"You sure?" he asked.

"Coach," I said, "do you want me to go to Oklahoma? Or Nebraska? Or Arkansas?" He laughed. "I don't want to go anywhere else," I said. "I'm committed."

"Have you told your dad yet?" Coach asked.

"No," I said, "I'm about to."

✦ ✦ ✦

When I told Dad I had committed to Colorado, he expectedly responded with some grumbling.

"You're going all the way to Colorado?" he said, shocked and surprised. "Why can't you go to LSU or Arkansas? I could drive right over and see you!"

"It's where I want to go," I said. "It's where I *need* to go."

I think he was disappointed that he was losing his little buddy. I had spent my entire life with him always by his side. There was not one thing we *didn't* do together. I think he was already going through withdrawals.

As for me, I was definitely sad that I would be leaving him. Not only was he my father; he was also my best friend. However, I was also excited to go to a place that had my heart. I knew without a doubt that I was making the right decision. It was the next step in my journey.

5

SNAKES OF BOULDER

My first year at the University of Colorado presented a brand new way of life.

New Orleans has amazing food, soul, culture, tradition and great people—people who are survivors, grinders, hustlers, and hard workers. People who are family-oriented and faith-oriented. The culture is always festive, fun, alive, and exciting.

Colorado is almost the opposite in some respects. It's more about nature and peace than culture and festivities. At the university, I often rode my bike on a path that went right through campus. It ran along a creek that was five or six feet deep, and the water was crystal clear. You could see fish swimming in the creek, like you were looking into an aquarium tank.

In a way, Colorado was like New Orleans's beautiful culture, tradition, and people translated into nature. Everything I had seen on the postcards, everything I had seen in the movies—it was all right in front of me. I'd seen postcards of the Rocky Mountains and people coming down the big slopes on skis or snowmobiles, and I'd seen vista points like what Paramount uses for its movies—and all of a sudden, I got to see it in person. It's supernatural—fifty-inch television screen supernatural. They have a golf course called The Sanctuary Golf Club there, and I can't think of a more accurate name for it.

From time to time, I'd drive the back roads that didn't have side rails through the mountains just to look out over the Rockies. I saw deer, elk, and raccoons all the time. From the Flatirons, I could see the entire university and all of Boulder. A herd of buffalo that were being raised and groomed were always sitting off the side of Interstate 70, going west through the mountains. I'd be up some five thousand feet, just looking out over all of those cliffs and thinking to myself, "Really?" *Really.*

It was just stuff like that—the experience of it all. It was a life I had never known. Words can't do Colorado justice. My freshman year at Colorado—despite the busyness of being a student-athlete—felt like a wonderful vacation to me, simply because of its scenery and its peacefulness.

The Flatirons, the foothills of the Rockies—that's my safe haven right there. It's the closest thing I know to heaven. We all have that place we go. Some guys like to go to their basement or their backyard; some guys go get a drink or go to the club. But I like relaxing away from everything. I like finding peace in Colorado.

✦ ✦ ✦

Like any freshman who leaves his home for the first time and goes off to school, my first year at school was eye-opening to me in a social sense. I think my favorite stories from my freshman year involve our junior linebacker, Chad Brown. Upon arriving in Colorado that summer, I immediately began attending some of Chad's parties at his off-campus apartment near Arapahoe Road in Boulder. I soon learned that Chad's apartment was the place to be on any given Friday or Saturday evening. Friends of the football team from all over the Boulder/Denver area gathered at Chad's in their baggy shirts, Duck Head pants, and Chuck Taylor sneakers, reflecting the Kris Kross style of the time. Some Colorado students, originally from the Los Angeles area—say, Compton or Watts—were always in attendance. Whatever the case, you really felt the West Coast flavor.

I think Chad's parties were popular not only because Chad was an awesome guy but also because he had a very intriguing place. "Intriguing" might be an understatement. It was unlike any other apartment anyone had ever seen. That's because it was filled with exotic snakes.

Seriously. Snakes.

I didn't know Chad all that well at the time—all I knew is that he had to be out of his darn mind. He seriously had ten to fifteen gigantic snake cages bordering the walls of his apartment! The first thing you saw when you walked into his apartment was a massive, white-and-yellow albino python, hanging in its cage, hissing. It always seemed like partygoers were hesitant to turn their backs to the cages, and it always seemed like there were a lot of people by the door. Chad promised us we were safe—that those nasty rodents, or whatever species they are, couldn't escape, but I'm not sure anyone believed him.

Anyway, those were Chad Brown's parties. To say the least, it was interesting coming from New Orleans—with its Southern, down-to-earth values, where you might ride your bike to your friend's front door just to make sure he made it home safely— and suddenly being in the mountains at a college party surrounded by exotic snakes. How does that work?

✦ ✦ ✦

As for football, I spent my freshman year as a backup quarterback behind Vance Joseph.

Our season-opener against Wyoming at home was unforgettable. One year before, I was watching the Buffaloes in awe on television, as they toppled over everyone in the country. And now I was a part of the defending national champions, proudly wearing the black and gold.

There's nothing like the tradition at the University of Colorado—staying at the College Inn with my teammates the night before and then making the ten- to fifteen-minute walk to the stadium beneath those beautiful blue and clear Colorado skies and eventually being led onto the Folsom Field by a gigantic, real-life buffalo named Ralphie. Tell me: what other football program in the country releases a wild animal from its cage and lets it make a lap around the field? No tradition comes close. Most teams have a student—a *person*—dressed up as a mascot, but we had a live animal! Once when we were taking team pictures, the photographers wanted some of us to get in Ralphie's cage. I didn't do that. Heck no.

I got on the field a couple of games that season—in blowout victories against Minnesota and Missouri at home—but my action was pretty minimal throughout the season. I don't think I attempted more than two passes that year. We finished 8–3–1 on the season and lost 30–25 to Alabama in the Blockbuster Bowl.

Overall, the season was a good transitional period for me. This was much-needed since I was going from high school football to one of the best collegiate programs in the country. It was surreal to be a part of the Colorado Buffaloes and have the chance to play on the field a couple times.

It helped me realize what it would take to fulfill my dream of starting at a Division I university and efficiently perform at that level. Because of Colorado's practices and workouts, I felt like I was able to develop as a player and as a quarterback, and I set myself up physically and mentally for what I hoped would be a solid sophomore campaign.

6

FOLSOM FRENZY

I stayed in Boulder the summer heading into my sophomore year. After moving to Colorado, I was hardly able to go home because flights were so expensive. I hated being away from Marrero for so long and especially hated being away from Dad, but there was no other solution. Colorado took care of me, however. Every Sunday throughout the summer, I went to church with Coach Simmons. He also helped me find summer jobs at Coca-Cola and Pepsi. Since I was making better money in Colorado than I would back in New Orleans, it made sense for me to work out west and assist my family financially from afar.

When I called home, Miss Dinah sometimes picked up the phone, and I remember her mentioning to me a few times that my father felt kind of—I wouldn't say depressed—but sad and lonely since I was no longer around. I would later learn from my father that my leaving was one of the most difficult things he has ever dealt with, outside of losing Momma.

I know it was a tough transition for my father to go from seeing me by his side almost every day to suddenly being thirteen hundred miles away. Whenever we talked on the phone, he would tell me how much he missed me. I missed him, too. And as fall approached, I hoped I could find a way to get him to Colorado to watch a football game and see his son.

My first start for the Buffaloes came in 1992, my sophomore season, when Coach McCartney gave me the nod over junior Vance Joseph and Duke Tobin (who went on to become one of the head scouts for the Cincinnati Bengals) in our season opener against our intrastate rival Colorado State. The game was in front of our home crowd. I felt some pressure that first game, but it also felt right. Colorado State had finished 3–8 the year before, and we had transitioned into a new offense during the offseason. A loss to our rival would have been an embarrassing blow, but I was ready to seize the opportunity. All those Colorado games I had watched my senior year of high school had led to that moment; now people were going to watch *me*. I hoped to give Buffalo Nation a glimpse of the quarterback and leader I knew I could be.

Entering the season, our offense had everything it needed to be successful. Lamont Warren was my tailback; and we ran a five-receiver set with guys like Michael Westbrook, Charles E. Johnson, Christian Fauria, and Erik Mitchell. We were stacked. Our offensive coordinator at the time, Les Steckel, had been a coach with the New England Patriots when they lost to the Chicago Bears in the 1985 Super Bowl—and he would go on to be Hall of Famer Shannon Sharpe's tight end coach in Denver. I loved learning from him.

The game against Colorado State started off relatively slow. I only had one hundred yards passing in the first half, but boy, once I got my feet wet, things got exciting. Bombs away, baby! I passed for three hundred yards in the second half and four hundred plus yards overall. To go from our slow start in the first half to our offensive explosion in the second half was extremely fulfilling. From the first half to the second half, from feeling nervous before the game to extremely confident by the end of the game—it was sort of a rags to riches storyline that gave Colorado faithful a taste of our potential and promise.

One pass I'll always remember is a sixty-yard bullet I threw to Charles E. Johnson *in stride*. That's what Coach Steckel always made me do in practice: throw passes as far as I could while my receivers ran as fast as they could. That's exactly what happened on that sixty-yard throw. Charles didn't have to change his stride, his arm motion, or anything! Throwing go-routes to Charles was the easiest thing in the world to do.

We won the game 37–17, and, to my surprise, in my first game starting, I broke the Colorado passing record that had stood for ten years. With my twenty-plus additional yards of rushing, I also broke the total yardage record that had stood for twenty-four years. I had four touchdown passes, tying a school record set by Darian Hagan during Colorado's national championship season, and I was named Big Eight Player of the Week and *Sporting News* Player of the Week.

Not a bad start to my college career.

The next week against Baylor, my success continued. I had three touchdowns and went 16-for-17 with 250-some yards in the first half. Unfortunately, I hurt my foot and couldn't play in the second half. Still, we won 57–38.

That week, I remember opening the local newspaper, the *Boulder Daily Camera*, and seeing my name listed second in the Heisman rankings behind San Diego State's Marshall Faulk. Unfortunately, my Heisman hopes soon ended because I had to sit out a couple games because of my foot.

✦ ✦ ✦

After spending all of October ranked in the Top 10, we finally lost our first game of the season against No. 8 Nebraska, falling to 6–1–1 on the season.

As good of a year as we had, the highlight of the season for me was that winter when the opportunity arose for my father to come out to Colorado for a game. He had never experienced anything like Colorado before. He might have seen a few snow flurries in Mississippi or something, but he had never experienced anything comparable to snowfall in the Rockies. The snow, the mountains, everything about that place was surreal to him.

One thing he didn't seem to enjoy, however, was the thin air. My dad was a smoker throughout much of his life, and many of our phone conversations my first two years at Colorado involved me encouraging him to quit. I cared deeply about him, and I wanted him to take better care of himself. Right when he arrived in Colorado, however, I witnessed him fall into a vicious coughing fit.

"Man," he said, "what in the world is going on?"

"It's the thin air, Dad," I said. "By the way, have you stopped smoking yet?"

"Yeah, yeah, yeah," he said, dismissing me, "I'm wearing the patch now."

He proceeded to remove his jacket and take a seat on the couch, as if trying to catch his breath. He then removed his CU-issued football cap, which he had been proudly sporting, and that's when a pack of cigarettes fell on the floor.

I think he was so overwhelmed with the coughing and the thin air that he completely forgot about the cigarettes in his cap.

"Gahhhd, dammit," he said.

We won our final three games of the season and entered the Fiesta Bowl in Tempe, Arizona, as the tenth-ranked team in the country. Unfortunately we fell to No. 6 Syracuse 26–22 and finished the season with a 9–2–1 record.

It had been a solid year, however; and in my first year as Colorado's starting quarterback, I hoped Colorado faithful caught a glimpse of the future and who we could become as a team.

7
FOOTBALL, A RELEASE

This is where things sped up.

My junior season was similar to my sophomore season. We finished the regular season 7–3–1 and entered the Aloha Bowl against No. 25 Fresno State as the seventeenth-ranked team in the country.

Being in Hawaii the week leading up to the game was especially fun. It was my first time in that beautiful state, and I remember our team keeping a close eye on the weather in Boulder to maintain some perspective. The people of Boulder were experiencing heavy snowfall all week, and we were enjoying eighty-five degree weather in Hawaii. Many of my teammates went out and rented mopeds to ride around the streets of Honolulu. I didn't because I was smart; I didn't want to get hurt. But we definitely took advantage of the warm weather while most Colorado faithful were stuck at home in a blizzard.

The game against Fresno was a shootout. Senior Trent Dilfer was at the helm of the Fresno offense, and he had a receiver named David Dunn who looked like Snoop Dogg with his braids. The two of them were a ridiculous offensive tandem. You'd think that Dilfer's 520-plus passing yards would have been enough to lead them to victory, but our offense was even more efficient. Our sophomore tailback, Rashaan Salaam, was bursting onto the scene, and he rushed for 130-plus yards and three touchdowns, earning him the Offensive MVP of the Aloha Bowl and leading us to a 41–30 victory. Rashaan was a shy, humble guy who came from eight-man football in San Diego, but boy was he electric on the field. Rashaan and I had quite the offensive tandem ourselves that year. He had nearly 1,000 rushing yards, and I had about 530 rushing yards along with 2,300 passing yards.

Anyway, the point is that we were locked and loaded on offense heading into my senior season, and we hoped we could do what the

Buffaloes had done in 1990: win another national championship for Coach McCartney and the good people of Boulder.

✦ ✦ ✦

Throughout my first three seasons at the University of Colorado, I received a couple of difficult phone calls from my family. One call informed me that my cousin David Patterson had passed away; another made me aware that his brother, Brian Patterson, had been murdered. This left Lisa, their sister, as the only surviving Patterson sibling. (For privacy concerns and out of respect for my extended family, I will not go into the details of their deaths.)

When I received the calls, I tried not to dwell too much on the horrifying news; I think that is why it is difficult for me to put it all into words today. In football, quarterbacks are taught to have short-term memory—you bottle things up the way you need to and deal with it the best you can; then you keep on going.

I don't say this to gloss over their deaths and the lives they lived. They were not distant family members who I only saw a couple of times; they were my cousins, some of my best friends with whom I hung out every weekend growing up. I saw them at church every Sunday, and almost every weekend we spent the night at one another's houses. A lot of times we found ourselves participating in some innocent mischief around the house that resulted in spankings. We probably deserved it.

It was weird to reflect on those times and realize that they were gone. Like losing my mom, it was difficult to understand. With it being beyond my control, I didn't know what else to do but to see it through and press on. Losing a family member is hard, but we all had to tell ourselves, "This too shall pass." I think it did.

The reason I say all this is because, one, it's something that not many people know about me, and two, it seemed to reinforce something I had felt since the passing of my mother—that football was an escape for me and an opportunity for me to experience joy and bring other people, particularly my family, joy as well.

8

THE CLIMB

We were out to prove something my senior season.

Offensively, we had all our weapons lined up. Entering the season, there was a debate amongst pundits about who would win the Heisman Trophy: Rashaan or me. Having two Heisman candidates on the same team was saying something, but that was just the tip of the iceberg. We had wide receiver Michael Westbrook and tight end Christian Fauria, who were both in their senior seasons and who went on to be drafted in the 1995 NFL draft. I could also throw to Phil Savoy, who had an outstanding college career, or Rae Carruth, or James Kidd, who both went on to play in the NFL. On the offensive line, we had guys like Chris Naeole, Bryan Stoltenberg, Tony Berti, Matt Lepsis, Heath Irwin, and Derek West, who all went on to play in the NFL as well. We had other weapons, too, but I don't want to bore you. I could go on for days about the quality of talent we had at Colorado during my years there, especially my senior season.

We also had a new quarterbacks coach my senior season in Rick Neuheisel, who had played quarterback at UCLA and who also mentored Troy Aikman as a coach at UCLA. On a personal level, Coach Neuheisel was great for me. He wanted to see me excel, he had mentored some of the best, and he had an understanding of what it took to play in the NFL. It was crazy that it was already time for me to be thinking about my future. My time at Colorado had flown by. I communicated to Coach Neuheisel that I wanted to be a quarterback in the NFL upon leaving Colorado, and he told me that he wanted to help me achieve this on an individual level but that it would be difficult.

According to Coach Neuheisel's friend, Leigh Steinburg, who I would later sign with as my agent, I was projected at the time to be the thirty-first rated quarterback in the 1995 Draft. Not thirty-first overall. The thirty-first *quarterback*. Though there might have been talk of me being a Heisman candidate, there were apparently some serious doubts from NFL scouts about my arm strength and my quarterbacking style, which some at the time might have considered unorthodox. They questioned whether my talents at quarterback would translate to the professional ranks. There were not many quarterbacks in the NFL with my style, nor were there many African-American quarterbacks in the NFL total.

It would take a meteoric rise to attain my dreams, but I had an entire season to make a statement. And, in some ways, it was just like I was back in Marrero playing against my brother and his older friends. I might have been the underdog, but I was determined to excel. Heading into the season, Coach Neuheisel and I adopted a kind of us-against-the-world mentality. We were on a mission as a team: to win a national championship. And I was on a mission as a quarterback: to play in the NFL.

✦ ✦ ✦

We definitely made a statement to start the season.

Entering the season ranked No. 8 in the country, we defeated Northeast Louisiana in our opener at home and followed that up with a dominant 55–17 victory against No. 10 Wisconsin at home. Our next game, against No. 4 Michigan at Michigan Stadium, would go down as the best game of my college career, and it involved one of the most memorable plays in the history of college football.

We were trailing 26–14 with five minutes left in the game against Michigan, we had given up seventeen unanswered points in the third quarter, and I had just fumbled on Michigan's goal line. I was sitting on the bench while Michigan had the ball, towel over my head in my own little world. I was worried because I didn't know if we'd have a chance to get the ball back again. I felt like my fumble had put our chances of winning in jeopardy.

Coach Neuheisel came up to me. He squatted down and put his hand on my knee. "Listen to me," he said. "Listen to me."

I looked at him.

"This is going to be the greatest comeback in college football history."

Behind us, members of the Michigan band were chanting, "Paper Champion! Paper Champion!" over and over, implying we were good on paper but not on the field.

I put my towel over my head as Coach Neuheisel walked away. He turned around and looked at me.

"You hear me?" he said firmly.

I nodded.

Michigan fumbled. Our offense took the field, and we drove seventy-two yards in a minute and a half, making the score 26–21.

I returned to the bench and put the towel over my head again, trying to block everything happening around me. Again, I hoped we would have another opportunity to get the ball. I hoped my two fumbles wouldn't cost us the game.

We attempted an onside kick, but Michigan recovered the football with 2:15 remaining. All Michigan had to do was get a first down to seal the victory. The game would have been over. But they didn't. They punted, and we took over with about fifteen seconds left.

I hit Michael Westbrook at our own thirty-six-yard line and spiked the ball to stop the clock with six seconds left. I began walking toward the sideline to regroup with our coaches and have a conversation about the next play.

"What are you doing?" Coach Neuheisel said, laughing as I walked toward the sideline. There was no sense discussing a play. There was only one play to run. I had to throw it deep.

I returned to the huddle, and I saw a desperate look in many of my teammates' eyes. Rashaan Salaam had his head down, praying. I gave all of them a look that said, "Here we go, fellas."

As we stepped up to the line of scrimmage, I noticed there were only three guys rushing us.

Only three rushers? I thought to myself. *This is a gift from heaven.*

I took the snap, dropped back to the twenty-seven-yard line, and threw the ball seventy yards toward the Michigan goal line. Blake Anderson tipped the ball at the two-yard line, it went into the end zone, and Michael Westbrook grabbed the ball over Ty Law for the touchdown and the win. I didn't see the touchdown because I lost sight of the ball before Mike grabbed it, but I saw Coach Mac run onto the field with his arms in the air, followed by the entire team.

There could be no doubts about my arm strength after a throw like that.

The Big House, Michigan's renowned stadium, went completely silent. You could have heard the proverbial pin drop. As I ran across the field toward the end zone in celebration, it was so quiet, I could hear myself breathing.

As we made our way to the tunnel after that game in Ann Arbor, Coach Neuheisel came up to me.

"I told you," he said. "Good job, kid."

Then he laughed and ran off.

✦ ✦ ✦

After the momentous victory against Michigan, we continued firing on all cylinders—defeating No. 16 Texas, Missouri, and No. 22 Oklahoma. As exciting as our start to the season was, what made me most happy had to do with my family.

Much like when my father had the opportunity to watch me play college football for the first time my sophomore year, my sister had the opportunity to watch me play college football for the first time my senior season when we played the Longhorns at the University of Texas, the week after the "Miracle at Michigan."

Though I don't remember much about my personal performance that game, I know my sister witnessed a good contest, because Rashaan Salaam broke the school rushing record with 362 yards. Regardless, it felt good to see her again for the first time in many years and to have her there to watch me play.

I didn't know it at the time, but that was the last game my sister ever saw me play.

✦ ✦ ✦

Heading into our seventh game of the season against No. 19 Kansas State, we had a dominant 6–0 record and were ranked No. 2 in the country. Coach Neuheisel believed that this matchup against the Wildcats and Chad May, their highly touted quarterback, might be an opportunity for me to seize the spotlight in front of a national television audience. Coach wanted to prove a point. So did I.

Our approach the entire season had been to knock the building down, brick by brick. In our six games, we had knocked off four ranked opponents. We wanted to prove that we were the best team in college football, and Coach Neuheisel and I wanted to show scouts that I had what it took to play professionally at an elite level. None of this was unrealistic because we were *rolling* as an offense, averaging forty-one points per game. I was playing well, our receivers were in sync, and Rashaan was emerging as the Heisman probable, on track to accumulate two thousand yards that season.

Rashaan and I often had a friendly competition during gamed to see who could reach one hundred rushing yards the quickest. Rashaan, of course, had the advantage because he got more touches, but one advantage I had was that I could pick up more yards if there was a hole or opening in the defense.

Against Kansas State, our silly competition continued. Tied with Kansas State 21–21 in the fourth quarter, I broke free down the sideline on an option play and exploded for a sixty-yard touchdown run, which ended up being the game-winning touchdown.

My teammates jumped all over me in pure elation. Already, it had been a magical season.

On the sideline, Rashaan slapped me on the side of my helmet and said, "Dude, bro, how did you cut up the sideline so fast?"

"I don't care how I did it," I said. "I'm just trying to get more rushing yards than you."

Rashaan started laughing. "I love you, man," he said.

I'm not saying that I *didn't* want to pitch it to Rashaan, but heck, if I *could* hold onto the football and gain more yards, I wasn't going to complain. Not that it mattered, anyway. I still usually lost. Rashaan was the best tailback in the country. He had 202 rushing yards that game, and I had 127 yards. I am pretty sure he hit the one hundred mark in the first half anyway. Maybe even the first quarter. I was determined that one of those days, I'd get him.

Unfortunately, we lost our following game on the road against No. 3 Nebraska, 24–7, which dropped us down to No. 7 in the polls. It was only one loss, against a good team nonetheless, but we were unable to work our way back up the polls to where we had once been. This was probably partially because our final three games of the season—against Oklahoma State, Kansas, and Iowa State—involved matchups against non-ranked teams.

However, the highlight of the season, in my opinion, came in the final week in our 41–20 victory against Iowa State—when Rashaan topped two thousand rushing yards on the season (2,055 total yards), breaking Colorado's single-season rushing record. At the time, he was only the fourth college running back to rush for more than two thousand yards.

When Rashaan topped two thousand yards, I remember my teammates hoisting him into the air at Folsom Field. As humble as he was, he wanted to get down. He didn't like being the center of attention. Of course, the boys would have none of that—such an accomplishment was worthy of being praised. Plus, he deserved the torture, especially after beating me in our little game week after week . . . after week after week.

Rashaan later approached me and said, "Thank you." He said he felt like we pushed one another each and every game and made one another better, which really made the offense thrive. I felt blessed to be on his team. It was a historical year for Colorado football, and Rashaan was the ideal teammate and friend. Turns out, we were only the second offense in Colorado's history to have a two-thousand-yard rusher, Rashaan, and two-thousand-yard passer, me, on the same team. It was on that same day that I became the all-time total offense leader in the Big Eight with 7,770 yards in my career. I felt fortunate to be a part of it all. I had the best weapons around me that a quarterback can imagine.

What made our offense so good my senior year were the unsung heroes on the offensive line—guys like Brian Stoltenberg, Heath Irwin, Chris Naeole, Toni Berti, Derek West—and tight ends like Christian Fauria and Matt Lepsis. That group of guys worked their butts off to protect me and Rashaan.

The day became even more dramatic at the post-game press conference when Coach McCartney announced to the media that he would be resigning at the conclusion of the season, after our bowl game. People were shocked, but I think that we, as players, had had a feeling from the start of the year that it might be Coach's final season.

That's one of the reasons why the seniors took it upon themselves week after week to approach the game with such dedication and determination. We wanted Coach to ride off into the sunset on a high note, like he deserved.

All in all, it was one of the wildest days of football you could possibly conceive. I could probably spend an entire chapter on that day alone.

One month later, Rashaan was named the sixtieth winner of the annual Heisman Trophy. (I finished thirteenth in the balloting) We had the best player in college football, we were headed to the Fiesta Bowl to take on the University of Notre Dame, and it was Coach Mac's final game at the helm of the Buffalo program. What a season.

✦ ✦ ✦

We still had a game to focus on, but it was around this time—during the month and a half between our final regular season game against Iowa State and our bowl game against Notre Dame—that I was introduced to Coach Neuheisel's friend, Leigh Steinberg. Leigh was yet to be my agent, but as I got to know him, I remember him asking me, "How do you feel about potentially playing a different position in the NFL?"

I looked him square in the eye and told him, "I want to be a quarterback."

Though our successful regular season had certainly benefited me, I apparently also had a long way to go. Leigh mentioned that if I could earn MVP honors at both the Fiesta Bowl and the Hula Bowl, a game featuring seniors from across the country, it would better my chances of getting drafted as a quarterback in the NFL. These two bowls were two big stage opportunities to show the country what I could do.

First and foremost, I wanted to win the Fiesta Bowl, which would be held in Tempe, Arizona—my second time in Tempe in three years. Winning the Fiesta Bowl would be the perfect way to cap off a historic season and conclude Coach Mac's ridiculously successful thirteen-year coaching career at Colorado, the coach with the most wins in Buffs history.

On a personal level, I kept those two goals in the back of my mind.

I knew it was crunch time and that my future as a pro football player was hanging in the balance.

✦ ✦ ✦

Our bowl game against Lou Holtz's Notre Dame squad wasn't even a contest. Late in the second quarter, we led 31–3, and we never looked back. Though the Irish made the score respectable, we held on for a 41–24 victory.

Obviously it would have been better if we could have sent Coach McCartney out with his second national championship; however, our loss earlier in the season to Nebraska, who went on to win the national championship, kept us out of the Orange Bowl. In today's college football playoff format, perhaps we would have been given a shot to win a national title. Who knows? To this day, when us Colorado Buffalo alumni get together, our 1994 team always argues with the 1990 national championship team about which squad was more talented. It will probably be a debate we have amongst ourselves until we're all gone.

Still, our 41–24 victory over Notre Dame in the Fiesta Bowl was a great way to send Coach Mac off into his post-football career—to ride out into the sunset with the joy of accomplishment that he deserved. It was the perfect conclusion to a near-perfect season.

Offensively, I went crazy in that game, amassing a season-high 348 yards of total offense. I was determined. After the game, I was named the Offensive MVP of the Fiesta Bowl, just as Leigh had told me I needed to do. It was a step in the right direction. Oh yeah, I also rushed for 140-plus yards compared to Rashaan's 80-plus yards. Take that, Rashaan.

✦ ✦ ✦

My girlfriend at the time, Jamie, went out to Hawaii with me at the end of January for the Hula Bowl (or the Senior Bowl). On our way to Hawaii, we met up with Leigh Steinberg in San Francisco to discuss the future. I reinforced to him my desire to be drafted into the NFL as a quarterback—and nothing else—and he once more encouraged me to make a statement in the Senior Bowl, just as I had done in the Fiesta Bowl. I remember Jamie telling me after the meeting, "Just fight for what you know and what you believe in. I'm with you."

A couple of good offensive drives solidified my naming of Offensive MVP in the Senior Bowl, and I remember thinking to myself, "Mission accomplished." I had done my job, hopefully making my future agent's job easier, and had showed NFL general managers across the country in the Fiesta Bowl and Hula Bowl that I could play the position.

I flew back to Colorado reflecting on the season, from the "Miracle at Michigan" (which would earn an ESPY for "College Football Play of the Year") to hoisting Rashaan in the air in Coach Mac's final game as head coach at Folsom Field. I was excited for my future, knowing I had just experienced four of the most incredible years in my life—alongside talented players, some of the most knowledgeable coaches, and the best of friends.

Soon after, I signed with Leigh Steinberg and began looking forward to my future, whatever it entailed.

I ultimately signed with Leigh because I trusted Coach Neuheisel's opinion about people. Coach had my best intentions in mind and believed in me. It seemed pretty self-explanatory to sign with Leigh considering his experience with guys like Troy Aikman, Drew Bledsoe, Steve Young, and particularly Warren Moon. Warren's success as an African American quarterback, who arose out of the ranks of the CFL and became a successful quarterback with the Houston Oilers, gave me the confidence that Leigh could do the same with me.

One day, Warren even called my apartment in Boulder to share his story with me and to talk to me about his relationship with Leigh. I have to admit, though I might not have seemed goo-goo-ga-ga when he called, I was most certainly goo-goo. "Stick to your ground," he told me, "believe in what you believe in; let it do what you do." What was interesting about this phase of my life, as I transitioned into my future career, is that never before in my life had I needed to decide what position I wanted to play or pursue. In high school, I was a quarterback because I was the best quarterback; in college, I was a quarterback because I was the best quarterback. My senior year heading into the NFL, however, I was at a crossroads of sorts because I knew that teams would be interested in signing me for a position other than quarterback. My conversation with Warren, however, once more encouraged me to stick to my guns.

"This is what I'm going to do," I remember thinking to myself. "I can't play anything else. Why should I have to change just because the masses might not be ready to see my style?"

I wasn't changing. I was determined, just as I had been all season.

9

MOMENT OF TRUTH

The spring of my senior year, I didn't go out and surround myself with a fancy team of trainers, coaches, or psychologists. I simply did what I had been doing for the last four years—I surrounded myself with my loving family at the University of Colorado. Why would I do anything else? They were the best. All those kind people were part of my maturation process, and it didn't make sense for me to turn my back on them; they were the reason why I had been so successful in the black and gold.

I conditioned with the team, under the direction of Coach Neuheisel who had accepted the head coaching position, and continued pushing myself and allowing them to push me. I was just as driven as I had been my senior year; my future had, in fact, become personal. Just like my senior year, I was out to prove a point. Today, they might talk about the McNabbs and the Vicks and the Kaepernicks and the Wilsons, but at that time, they were not. Was the NFL prepared for my talent though they didn't often see it? I indeed had an arm—I wasn't a Wildcat-style quarterback, but I also wasn't your typical pocket-passer. Was the NFL ready?

It helped Leigh to know that my being drafted as a quarterback was non-negotiable, because it affected how we went through the process leading up to the draft.

Chicago wanted to try me out as a tailback because I had a forty-yard dash time that was as fast as Michael Westbrook's, a 4.39. Indianapolis wanted to try me out at tailback, too. I didn't return the interest. "No, I'm good," I told them both.

When general manager Tom Donahue and the Steelers approached me at the combine, it was a bit different. They knew I wanted to play quarterback. They knew that was my passion. But, because of my skill set, they wondered if I would be willing to help them out at other positions if they needed me to. "Yes," I told them, because they understood that my desire was to be a quarterback.

The thought of playing for Pittsburgh got me really excited. Five players from the University of Colorado were with the Steelers— Charles E. Johnson, Deon Figures, Ariel Solomon, Joel Steed, and Chad Brown. Playing for the Steelers seemed like it might be an extension of my festive days in Boulder.

The 1995 NFL Draft was held on April 22. I didn't get picked up the first round early that day and was passed up by Minnesota and Jacksonville, two teams who were very interested in me. Between three o'clock and five o'clock that day, I remember sitting next to Jamie on the couch in her apartment and receiving a call from Mr. Donahue.

"Kordell, how ya doing, buddy?" Mr. Donahue said.

"I'm doing well," I said.

"I'm here on the phone with Coach Cowher and all the coaches," Mr. Donahue continued. "How would you like to play football for the Pittsburgh Steelers?"

"I would love that," I responded. "Thank you. Thank you for the opportunity."

After the phone call, I hugged Jamie and we cried tears of joy.

We had done it. I couldn't believe I'd gone from being the thirty-first-rated quarterback in the draft to being the fourth quarterback selected with the sixtieth pick by the Steelers. We had completed the climb. Leigh would later tell me he had never seen a quarterback climb the draft board in a year's time like that before.

Pittsburgh gave me a No. 10 jersey—a quarterback's number—and welcomed me to the team. It felt like I was flying high.

I couldn't have been happier.

And I was very thankful.

PART II

STEELERS

10

SLASH

I had never spent any time in Pittsburgh before. The only thing I knew about Pittsburgh was that one of my roommates in college always called it "Shitsburgh." He said he called it "Shitsburgh" because "the weather was always shitty." Of course, he was comparing Pittsburgh to Boulder, Colorado—the only two places he had ever spent much time. Can you blame him? The rivers of the Allegheny, Monongahela, and Ohio that run through Pittsburgh are brown— the creeks that run through Boulder are as clear as Fiji water!

When I showed up in Pittsburgh for OTAs and training camp, however, I thought it was beautiful. Granted, it wasn't winter, but I was immediately drawn to the city. Entering Pittsburgh through the Fort Pitt tunnel beneath Mount Washington and exiting to be immediately greeted by the city's spectacular skyline was unforgettable. Making that drive at night and seeing all the buildings alight along the Monongahela is even more etched in my memory.

Upon arriving at Three Rivers Stadium for the first time, there along the banks of the Allegheny, I couldn't help but think about how historical of a stadium I was about to be practicing and playing in on a consistent basis. I thought about the Steelers' battles with the Dallas Cowboys I had learned about in my youth, or the Immaculate Reception against the Oakland Raiders in 1972 when I was born, or legends like Terry Bradshaw, Franko Harris, Joe Gilliam, Mark Malone, "Bubby" Brister, Lynn Swann, and "Mean Joe" Greene—and I could go on and on. It seemed like yesterday that I'd been a little kid playing pick-up football in Marrero with my brothers' friends or playing that tabletop electric football game with my family. And now, here I was, in the NFL.

My first time walking into the Steelers' facility, I noticed all the history. I saw the Steelers' four championship trophies from the 1970s and the giant picture of Old Man Rooney behind the front desk. It was a football enthusiast's paradise. I ate it up, my memories reminding me of that amazing era in football.

And then, just like that, it was time to go to work.

✦ ✦ ✦

My relationship with Steelers head coach Bill Cowher began during training camp in 1995. He had been the Steelers' next hire after the legendary Chuck Noll and had been with the organization since 1992. I liked Coach Cowher. He got the most out of his players, and he made me feel comfortable right away.

The Steelers' starting quarterback in 1995 was veteran Neil O'Donnell—one of my favorite quarterbacks of all time—who had been with the Steelers since 1990. Not only was Neil a talented quarterback; he was also a caring individual who befriended me when I moved to Pittsburgh. We were actually neighbors (he lived six houses down from me), and I sometimes hung out with him, his wife, and their chocolate Labrador.

As I went through preseason training camp and entered the 1995 regular season, it was obvious to me that I needed to learn as much from Neil as possible. That's because I started the season as a fourth-string quarterback behind Neil, veteran Mike Tomczak, and second-year Jim Miller. Most teams don't even carry four quarterbacks, but the Steelers did in 1995. My role on the team was to stand on the sideline in khaki shorts and carry around a clipboard.

At least for a time.

✦ ✦ ✦

I was different than most quarterbacks when I warmed up. Whereas Neil, Mike, and Jim had a receiver stand next to them to catch the football and hand it to them, I liked running around and catching the football and then throwing it back.

One day in practice, Neil and I were warming up together, and he said to me, "You look like you can catch."

I began running side to side in order to give him a moving target, just as a receiver would do. Our offensive coordinator Ron Erhardt was standing nearby. "Coach," I told him, "I'll help out at other positions if y'all need me to."

Over time, I ended up telling Coach Cowher and our wide receivers coach Chan Gailey the exact same thing. "Instead of me just rotting away doing nothing," I told them, "I want to get busy."

A few weeks later, after injuries to receivers Charles E. Johnson and Johnnie Barnes, Coach Cowher began seriously considering playing me at receiver.

One day we had a meeting in his office, and he asked me, "What do you think about it?"

"I'm good with it," I told him, "as long as I have my opportunity to compete for the starting quarterback job in the future. And as long as I can keep No. 10."

"Let's do it," he said.

If it weren't for injuries, I probably wouldn't have played a down my rookie season. But we were battered and bruised on offense. And after starting the season with a 3–4 record—a record that, for Pittsburgh, brings with it a feeling that the world is coming to an end—we were looking for *anything* to get back on the winning trail. "Anything," as I would find out, included Coach Cowher reporting me as a third-string quarterback and using me at various positions.

The first time I touched the ball in an NFL game was in the eighth game of the season against the Jacksonville Jaguars at our home field, Three Rivers Stadium. I entered the game prepared to run a quarterback draw. It was third and long, and we were in a five-receiver set—we called it "Buffalo Personnel." I took the snap, tucked the ball, and ran. Right up the middle. *First down.*

Three Rivers exploded.

We beat Jacksonville 24–7 that week to improve to 4–4, and I had two rushes for sixteen yards. I didn't do much the next week, but I got a couple touches, and we defeated the 6–2 Chicago Bears 37–34 in overtime. It was a momentous win because it was the first time the Steelers had *ever* beaten Chicago in Chicago.

All that mattered was that we were winning. After a difficult start, there was a sense that the season could turn into something magical.

✦ ✦ ✦

The following week against the Cleveland Browns, the floodgates opened.

I had two rushes for thirteen yards in that game and two catches at wideout for twenty-one yards. Because Coach Cowher reported me as a third-string quarterback, I was able to line up as a receiver with a headset in my helmet. This was extremely beneficial to me. As a rookie, I was still learning the Steelers' complex, in-depth offensive playbook, and the headset allowed me to hear the play *twice*: immediately through the headset from the coaches and once more when Neil called out the play in the huddle. This was invaluable for me and helped my learning curve.

At one point during the game, we were in the red zone and I took the snap from the shotgun on a designed bootleg right. Everything was covered, so I then reversed field and found wide receiver Ernie Mills in the back of the end zone. It was my first completion in the NFL and my first touchdown.

That moment was followed by sheer pandemonium.

As I ran to the sideline, a lot of my teammates met me on the fifty-yard-line and celebrated with me. The crowd was going wild. It was crazy for me to consider that I was even getting a chance to play considering where I'd been on the depth chart at the start of the season.

Many say that was *the* game, a 20–3 victory against the Browns, when "Slash" was born.

I was just having fun.

Like I was a kid again.

✦ ✦ ✦

I felt like I took another step forward in the offense the following week against the Cincinnati Bengals on the road. I really started to build chemistry and trust with Neil.

Down 31–13 early in the second half, we knew we needed to kick it into high gear. We had already lost to Cincinnati by eighteen points earlier in the year, and we were looking to strike back. We did.

We closed the gap in the third quarter and entered the fourth quarter trailing 31–28. All day, I felt like I had been open and was being overlooked. As a quarterback, knowing how it makes a quarterback feel when receivers tell you they are open, I expressed my concerns to backup Mike Tomczak instead.

"Mike," I said, "listen, you *have* to tell Neil I'm wide open." He apparently told him because on a play in one of our next drives, I lined up in the slot and took off down the middle. Neil threw it to me, and I caught it, pulled a spin move on Bengals safety Darryl Williams, and took off down the field. Seventy-one yards. *Touchdown.* All of a sudden, after being embarrassed one quarter before, we had the lead. We went on to win 49–31; at the time, it was the second biggest comeback in Steelers history.

It was like we couldn't lose.

After starting the season 3–4, we went on an eight-game tear: 24–7 over Jacksonville, 37–34 over Chicago, 20–3 over Cleveland, 49–31 over Cincinnati, 20–17 over Cleveland again, 21–7 over Houston, 29–10 over Oakland, and 41–27 over New England. We won five games in the fourth quarter that season and one game in overtime. Steeler Nation was buzzin'.

It was almost as if that little wrinkle—how Coach Gailey and Coach Erhardt incorporated "Slash" into the offense—helped us get over the hump. It created diversions on offense and helped take the pressure off Neil. We were one of the first teams in the league to run a five-receiver set on offense, and when you mix that with some misdirection and creativity, it was as if Neil was at a smorgasbord. He had the pick of the litter. Defenses had no idea what to do against us.

As for me, in a matter of weeks, I had gone from a fourth-string quarterback to a Steeler Nation phenomenon. It was a surprise to me, but I took it in stride. What's funny is that whenever my father and I were together, we never even talked about the excitement of my rise that season. It was as if we both just knew that what we always hoped would happen had indeed finally happened. It reminded me of what he always told Miss Dinah: "If my boy keeps doing what he's doing, he's going to play in the pros!" Well, here I was. He was right.

Much like the shock I experienced when I realized the University of Colorado was recruiting me, I experienced the same rush of excitement as the good people of Pittsburgh got excited about my abilities. There were No. 10 Steelers jerseys *everywhere*, and I hadn't even *touched* the ball until halfway through the season!

Like being a Buffalo in college, I felt loved as a Steeler.

Oh, to be loved by Pittsburgh . . . well, there's no love like it.

✦ ✦ ✦

We lost our final game of the regular season but had already clinched the AFC Central with an 11–5 record. The last time we had lost a game was all the way back in mid-October. What we had in 1995 was a special and resilient group. Those guys were my family. I was a small part of our success, but boy was it a memorable ride!

In the first round of the playoffs, we defeated Thurman Thomas and Jim Kelly's Buffalo Bills 40–21 to advance to the AFC Championship game against the Indianapolis Colts. Being in the AFC Championship game was crazy in itself. And Indianapolis had their quarterback Jim Harbaugh, nicknamed the "Comeback Kid," as well as Lamont Warren, who had been my tailback at the University of Colorado, backing up Marshall Faulk.

At the end of the first half, we trailed the Colts 6–3 at Three Rivers and were in the Colts' red zone. Neil hiked the ball, and I ran a slant on the backside but was double-covered by the linebacker and safety. Neil started scrambling, and, having scrambled plenty myself as a quarterback, I shifted directions in my route and cut back to the right where Neil could make an easy throw to me in the end zone. I was wide open, and he threw it to me. *Touchdown.*

It ended up being a critical touchdown in our momentum, and we went on to defeat the Colts 20–16. For the first time in sixteen years (back in Terry's Bradshaw's era), the Steelers organization was going to the Super Bowl.

✦ ✦ ✦

I surprised my dad with a ticket to the Super Bowl in Tempe, Arizona, and he was in seventh heaven. He loved having the opportunity to go.

Strangely, I had also gone to Tempe for our bowl game when I was a sophomore in college and again when I was a senior. The Super

Bowl made it three times in four years. When we arrived in Arizona, I was saying to myself, *Is this how it's supposed to be? Going back to Arizona every year?*

In a way, it almost seemed too easy.

Not only was I going to the Super Bowl my rookie season, but I was also playing in one of the most classic Super Bowl rivalries imaginable: the Dallas Cowboys vs. the Pittsburgh Steelers, two teams that had played in two unforgettable Super Bowls in the 1970s. Both the Steelers and Cowboys entered the game with the opportunity to tie the San Francisco 49ers for the most Super Bowl wins by any franchise: five.

It was the ride of my life. I was just happy to play. It was crazy that there were six of us from the University of Colorado on that team: me, Charles E. Johnson, Ariel Solomon, Joel Steed, Chad Brown, and Deon Figures. It felt like family. On top of that, we had guys like Greg Lloyd, Kevin Greene, Justin Strzelczyk, Jerry Olsavsky, Brenden Stai, John Jackson, Tom Newberry, Willie Williams, and Hall of Famers Rod Woodson and Dermontti Dawson. I could go on and on about the talent we had. To top things off, one of my favorite quarterbacks—and human beings, for that matter—Neil O'Donnell, led us there. Having all this talent somehow work together as a cohesive unit was extremely exciting.

I remember sitting in my hotel room in Tempe, thinking about the fact that I was playing *with* all these great players for a legendary organization and going *against* all these other great players, like Troy Aikman, Emmitt Smith and Deion Sanders, who played for another legendary organization. Seriously. In my first year!

Coach Cowher was great that whole year—and he was great during the Super Bowl. It was his first Super Bowl, too. We were all experiencing it together. He told us just to play and enjoy the moment.

Unfortunately, the game didn't turn out the way we hoped. Dallas jumped to a 13–0 lead before we scored a touchdown at the end of the half. In the second half, Cowboys cornerback Larry Brown had two interceptions, which Dallas turned into touchdowns, and Brown became the first cornerback to be named Super Bowl MVP. We lost 27–17. What's interesting is that Neil, though he had three interceptions in the game, entered the Super Bowl as the NFL's all-time leader in fewest interceptions per pass attempt.

However, on a positive note, the season turned out much better than it had begun, both for me personally and for the team as a whole. I went from a fourth-string quarterback to the Steelers' Rookie of the Year, and our team started the 1995 season with an abysmal 3–4 record and then reached the Super Bowl.

As I reflect on that season today, I'm reminded of the promise I felt during my early days in Pittsburgh—the promise for the players, coaches, and me. Never in my wildest dreams had I expected to reach the Super Bowl that year or even to be a contributor after carrying around a clipboard for the first seven games.

I felt favor in Pittsburgh. I felt like I was a part of the team. It all felt right. I knew I could play in the NFL, I knew I belonged there, and I still knew I belonged at quarterback. All I needed was a shot.

✦ ✦ ✦

Like Colorado, Pittsburgh felt like home. Like in Colorado, I was just having fun that first year in Pittsburgh. I felt like a cartoon character: *Slash*. Like I was Batman in a comic book. Run! *Boom!* Catch! *Pow!* Throw! *Hazam!*

Slash.

It may be a weird way to explain it, but that's the best way I know to describe that first season. And I couldn't wait to see what my future as a Steeler would entail.

11

THE CALL IN SEWICKLEY HEIGHTS

Heading into my second season with the Steelers, I received a call from my father. Sometimes I drove through the borough of Sewickley Heights on the northwest side of Pittsburgh to look at the beautiful houses on my way home from practice, and this was one of those days. "Kordell," my father said in a voice that was reminiscent of Falisha's cautious approach when she told me Momma had passed away when I was eleven. "Your sister isn't doing too good. I think you need to come home."

I immediately turned around and went back to the facility to tell Coach Cowher and Coach Gailey in person that I wouldn't be at practice that week because I needed to see my sister. I found the next flight I could to New Orleans and flew home.

Two years before, when Falisha had attended the game against Texas my senior season, she'd been in the middle of battling an incurable disease that had been slowly chipping away at her health. As I entered my second season with the Steelers, the disease pulled her into a very weak state, similar to the condition my mother had been in when she attended Falisha's graduation. (I recognize I have not been very detailed in describing instances of loss and sickness within my family, but out of respect for my loved ones, I will refrain from diving into specifics. Still, I know these instances are a part of my story and have made me the person I am today, so I have touched on them to the best of my ability.)

When I arrived in New Orleans, I noticed how different Falisha looked, and all I could do was think to myself, "Dang." This was not the same healthy, vibrant Falisha I had always known. She was a deathly sick, and it was obvious she didn't have much time left.

I hated seeing her like that, and to this day, that period of my life is a blur and both difficult and painful to recall. Four days before training camp in 1996, Falisha passed away. And not long after my sister passed away, another one of my cousins, Kevin McDaniel, also passed away.

✦ ✦ ✦

In the movie *Blade: Trinity*, there is a powerful scene with Blade (played by Wesley Snipes) and Abigail Whistler (played by Jessica Biel). Drake, the antagonist, kills a blind woman named Sommerfield, and Abigail discovers her body. As Abigail holds Sommerfield's body and cries, Blade stands behind her and says two powerful words: "Use it."

Abigail continues to cry, and Blade says it again in a deep voice, "*Use* it."

Her tears keep falling, and he says it one more time, "*Use* it."

Blade is trying to tell Abigail to take the pain and anguish she feels in the moment and "use it" to help him kill Drake, the enemy. His point is for her to take something negative and use the energy toward something positive, to take all that she is feeling and use it to impact someone or bring joy to someone else. The death of her dear friend was something that was uncontrollable; the only thing she could control was her response to the tragedy.

Though the movie didn't get great reviews, this scene has always resonated with me. We've all experienced hardship on some level, and we all have a choice as to how we respond. Will we sulk in our sorrows? Or will we use them to impact others and leave a mark on this world? Will we be victims? Or will we be victors?

12

SLASHING SLASH

The 1996 season was a transitional season for us at quarterback. After losing to Dallas in the Super Bowl in 1995, Neil O'Donnell was picked up by the New York Jets. Some have theorized that Neil's three interceptions in the Super Bowl were ultimately his death knell in Pittsburgh—something that ultimately led to the Steelers to not extend his contract in the offseason, thus paving the way for me. It's an interesting theory, but the reality is that it was heartbreaking at the time to make it so far and fall short.

Heading into the season, Mike Tomczak—a veteran quarterback who had spent eleven years in the league playing for the Bears, Packers, and Browns—was named the starting quarterback, but I was told that I would be utilized more at the quarterback position, particularly in red zone opportunities, while continuing to play my role as Slash.

I think Coach Cowher liked the whole Slash phenomenon. It seemed like he enjoyed the opportunity to be creative as a head coach. Between Mike and myself, the coaches developed the only two-quarterback rotation in the league at the time. Each week at practice, he would draw up special plays for me that we would reveal on game day.

What was unique was that the coaches mostly had me taking snaps in the red zone. Mike would get us all the way down the field, and then I would come in and score the touchdown. One of our teammates, a linebacker named Levon Kirkland who had a very entertaining personality, would always kid with me and say to Mike, "How can you take it, bro? You do all that work going ninety yards, and this little punk whippersnapper gets all the glory for all the work you did!" If I scored a touchdown, Levon might say to me, "How can you feel good about yourself, bro?" Of course, he was kidding.

Perhaps the biggest pickup for our offense in 1996 was a running back from the St. Louis Rams named Jerome Bettis. He later told me that one of the reasons he came to Pittsburgh was because of my opportunity to be a starter. Apparently he could see us working well together.

That was some good foresight because we became great teammates and even better friends. His first year with the Steelers, in fact, we began a tradition and started playing golf together whenever we could. We tried to play multiple times a month, if not every week, and it would get pretty competitive. I usually gave him four or five strokes per side, and we always adjusted the handicap heading into the back nine. It was a pretty serious system because we were playing for serious money. Full disclosure, I took that poor man's money on the golf course for years. It's not that I was a good golfer at the time, but Jerome was definitely a bad golfer at the time.

Over the years, however, Jerome started getting better and better. And now, in our post-football careers, he takes my money every time we play. What's worse is that after giving him strokes all those years and trying to help him out, he refuses to give me any strokes today! And this man is supposed to be my friend! My son likes colorful socks and colorful soccer cleats, but I can't buy them because Jerome takes my money. This is money that could be used to make memories with my son at Disney World, the friendliest place in the world, but I can't take him there because Jerome takes my money. And this man is supposed to be my friend!

In all seriousness, Jerome Bettis is a good guy with a good heart. I am humbled to call him my friend, and I was excited when he came to the Steelers in 1996. I couldn't wait to see what we could do together.

Toward the end of the '96 season, Mike started to struggle at quarterback, and I ended up splitting time with him during our two playoff games. I enjoyed marching down the field with the offense and not just trying to get into the end zone from the red zone as I had done all year.

Unfortunately, we ended our season with a 28–3 loss to the Patriots in the Division Championship, one of the foggiest games I've ever played. One positive note at the conclusion of the season was that I was named a Pro Bowl alternate at wide receiver. It was interesting to be recognized at a position that I didn't even want to play the rest of my career. Our running backs coach at one point even told me that he believed I could be a Hall of Fame receiver. It was a compliment—it really was—but my response to him was, "Why not a Hall of Fame quarterback?"

As fun as being Slash was, I never took my eyes off of what I truly wanted. I was happy to do anything Coach Cowher needed me to do, but I still had goals. And my goal was not to be a quarterback-*slash*-running back-*slash*-wide receiver-*slash*-punter the rest of my career. I was happy to do it, and it was a blast, but my goal was to be a quarterback.

And not just any quarterback. The starting quarterback for the Pittsburgh Steelers.

✦ ✦ ✦

The offseason of 1997 was another transitional period. After losing to the Patriots in the 1996 playoffs, cornerback Rod Woodson, one of the town's favorite players, went to the San Francisco 49ers. We also lost Chad Brown, Ernie Mills, Andre Hastings, Deon Figures, and Brentson Buckner that year. Our team looked entirely different than it did when we'd gone to the Super Bowl two seasons before.

On the quarterback side, it became clear after a great preseason that I had won the starting position, and I was finally given my shot—a shot to fulfill my dream of being a successful starting quarterback for an NFL franchise.

My time had finally come.

✦ ✦ ✦

Being named the starting quarterback was a great privilege, but it also felt much more like a job—a serious responsibility with real consequences. I was under the microscope, the telescope, or whatever scope you wanted to call it. Everything was intensified. It was like having to go to work. *It's business now, buddy.*

As Slash, I could drop a pass here and there and not get booed. What I did as Slash—the excitement my unique role added to the game—felt like a bonus to Steeler Nation. To fans, I was a surprise every week. A wildcard. But if I had a bad game as quarterback . . . boy, I knew the pressure would be intense.

Being Slash in 1995 and 1996 turned out to be invaluable for my confidence as I entered the 1997 season. Though I wasn't a starting quarterback those seasons, I felt beloved and accepted by Pittsburgh. I was one of their own. This gave me a lot of security when I took over the quarterback role. I couldn't wait to bring people joy as I showcased my abilities at quarterback, just as I had hopefully brought them joy as Slash.

Entering the season, everything felt new and exciting. The team looked entirely different, and we were introducing a new style of quarterbacking to a town that was used to traditional pocket quarterbacks from Terry Bradshaw to Neil O'Donnell and Mike Tomczak. Sure, there was "pressure," too. Coach Cowher had taken the Steelers to the playoffs in his first five seasons—four with Neil and one with Mike—and I didn't want to be the first of his quarterbacks to not make a postseason appearance.

However, I saw it all as an *opportunity* rather than as *pressure*—an opportunity to finally play a position I felt I was meant to play in the NFL, an opportunity to be a leader and build on the Steelers' recent successes.

13

MY TIME

The 1997 season didn't start out the way I hoped.

In our first game, we got smoked 37¬–7 by the Cowboys at home. It was the first time we had played the Cowboys since my rookie season, when we'd lost to them in Super Bowl XXX. There were just too many things in that game that were out of sync. It didn't help that I had a slight MCL tear in my left knee and was required to wear a knee brace, which didn't allow me to be as elusive as I had been in my role as Slash.

The next week against the Washington Redskins wasn't much better offensively. I was still wearing a brace because of the slight tear in my knee, but we ended up lucking out with a couple of Washington turnovers and a drive in the final minutes and won 14–13.

After a bye, Week 4 presented another opportunity to make a statement—this time on Monday Night Football against the Jacksonville Jaguars. But we fell 30–21to the Jags and slipped to 1–2 on the season—a start that very easily could have been 0–3.

It was kind of a nightmare start, honestly—especially after feeling as if I couldn't do anything wrong the first two years. I suppose it was a reality check. However, I never questioned whether I should have remained in my "Slash" role; I wanted to prove I could work just as hard at quarterback and lead the team to victory.

The next week, we beat the Tennessee Oilers 37–24. Entering Week 6 against the Baltimore Ravens, I knew we had an opportunity to gain confidence and momentum if we could pull off a victory against our archrival.

✦✦✦

Our game against Baltimore was a big game for us. We were 2–2 on the season, we were on the road, and the organization was still deciding if they were in favor of the "Kordell Experiment" or if they liked me better in the Slash role. Our offense was new, so some grace was extended there. But there was also pressure for our system to work.

The game, however, began as horribly as I could have imagined. I threw two interceptions in the first quarter and another at the start of the second quarter. In other words, in our first three possessions, I threw *three* interceptions. Heading into that game, I had three interceptions on the season; now here I was with three interceptions in *one half*. Words can't explain how frustrated I was. We trailed 14–0 at the end of the first quarter and gave up another touchdown in the second quarter.

"What do you have to lose now?" Coach Cowher told me on the sidelines. "You screwed it up, kid . . . so hey, go fix it! You owe me one!"

He said it in a comforting way—a way that alleviated some of the pressure and helped my mind feel free. His comment helped me accept the three interceptions for what they were and move on. He was right; I had performed horribly at the start. But what was there to lose now?

We finally got on the board when I went on a one-yard run up the middle for a touchdown with about seven minutes left in the half.

They scored a field goal at the end of the first half, and we went into the locker room trailing 24–7.

When we took the field again for the second half, an ex-teammate of mine who was playing for Baltimore came up to me and said, "I told you," as if saying, "See, I told you we'd win."

"Game's not over," I told him.

Our returner, Will Blackwell, started the second half off right with a ninety-seven-yard kickoff return for a touchdown, and midway through the third quarter, I threw a touchdown pass to get us to within three points. It was 24–21, with all the time in the world left to play.

"That's one," I told Coach Gailey on the sideline via phone.

"You've got a lot more to go," he said. "You're not done yet."

After punting on our first possession in the fourth, I threw another touchdown on the following drive to give us our first lead of the game, 28–24.

"That's two," I told Coach Gailey.

On our next drive, I threw for another touchdown, my fourth since we'd trailed 21–0 early on. And since their early lead, Baltimore had yet to answer to one of our touchdowns.

"That's three," I told Coach Gailey again.

I was extremely exhausted by this time. It was one of those games where you walk through the valley and climb to the mountain, all in sixty minutes.

Baltimore didn't go down without a fight, though; they scored their first touchdown of the second half with about three minutes left in the game. They were successful on the two-point conversion to make the score 35–32, and their fans grew excited and loud for the first time since the second quarter.

On our next possession, we faced a third-and-four on our own twenty-six-yard line. Baltimore had a chance to force us to go three-and-out, and the fans at Memorial Stadium were so loud it was deafening.

Earlier in the game, our running backs coach, Dick Hoax, had noticed that Baltimore's defense ignored me on a reverse, so Chan Gailey drew up a play for me to keep the ball on third down and run for the first down. We got much more than the four yards needed for a first down, however. I broke free, ran seventy-four yards into the end zone, and capped it off with the Nestea Plunge. I was feeling it. We had completed our comeback and secured the win.

"That's four," I told Coach Gailey, laughing. "You think that's enough?"

"It may be enough," he joked. "I don't know. But great job today. You can relax yourself now."

On the sidelines following the touchdown, Coach Cowher started looking for me, asking everybody where I was. At this time, my quad was hurting from an injury I'd gotten the week before. As I walked over to Coach Cowher, limping, he said, "What's wrong, kid?"

"I hurt my quad on the run," I said.

"But you scored, right?" he said.

"Yep," I replied.

"Great job today, kid," he said, hugging me like I was his own child, then kissing me on the cheek. "You got yourself in a hole, and you got yourself out of it."

He had the biggest smile I had ever seen on his face. We were both caught up in the euphoria of it all—from three interceptions to four touchdowns, from embarrassment to victory against our rival on the road.

✦ ✦ ✦

Those types of wins became a trend that season. It wasn't always pretty. But we got it done. Always.

Following Baltimore, we won eight of our final eleven regular season games. Three of those victories were overtime wins. Three of them! Things always seemed to come down to the wire, but we'd grind it out and usually get the victory. No one in the NFL seemed to perform better down the stretch than us.

Just like our Super Bowl season, we were rolling.

For me, there was more responsibility. A little bit more pressure. But at the end of the day, it was a *game*. I was getting paid to play a *game*. And I loved having the opportunity to be a leader.

Much like in 1995, our Super Bowl season, when we'd had a slow start and it had taken me several weeks to break into the lineup, it took a few weeks for us to get going in 1997, too. Once we found our groove, however, we were unbeatable. We just kept winning. And winning. And winning.

I felt as if I had seized the opportunity, embraced the pressure, and successfully proved the doubters wrong. I felt as if I had become a fixture in Pittsburgh. Being Slash was great, but leading the Steelers was even better.

Perhaps our biggest victory of that regular season came in Week 16 against the New England Patriots, who had knocked us out of the playoffs the year before. Heading into Foxboro and going up against a team with a 9–5 record (we were 10–4), we knew it was crucial to get a win because a victory would give us a bye and home field advantage throughout the playoffs.

It was a big game—a game I'll always remember. First off, it was another one of our overtime games, and from the Patriots' perspective, it never should have gone into overtime. The Pats led 14–0 in the first half, and it seemed like they had buried us when their running back Dave Meggett scored a fifty-yard touchdown with four minutes remaining in the game, giving them a 21–13 lead.

They took possession again with three minutes remaining. They only needed one first down to run out the clock. That's when quarterback Drew Bledsoe threw a pick to our lineman Kevin Henry.

On our possession, we ended up facing a fourth down on New England's fifteen-yard line before I threw a completion to Yancey Thigpen and an eventual touchdown to our tight end Mark Bruener, making the score 21–19. We tied it 21–21 with a two-point conversion.

In overtime, our kicker Norm Johnson hit a thirty-one-yard field goal to secure the victory. It was wild. Improbable. I remember one of the Patriots players telling the press that the loss hurt worse than their Super Bowl loss to the Packers the year before.

✦ ✦ ✦

Much like the previous season, Coach Cowher was having fun, I was having fun, and Pittsburgh was having fun. Coach Cowher was trying something new in Pittsburgh: me. The foundation of our relationship was creativity and excitement.

First, he innovatively used me as Slash; no other coach in the league was doing anything quite like that. Then he gave *me*, an unconventional quarterback in Pittsburgh's pocket-passing history, an opportunity as the starting quarterback for the Steelers; no other coach was doing that either.

We were having an incredible ride together—breaking barriers and captivating Steeler Nation. It really did feel like we were Pittsburgh's "Dynamic Duo." I had a unique set of talents, and Coach Cowher used them to perfection. I was like the jack-in-the-box that Coach Cowher wound up and released. We seemed inseparable at the time because of what we had accomplished together. We had a bond—a strong one. Heck, we were even in a Footaction commercial together. In the commercial, I threw a football across the field, hitting Coach Cowher in the head. Then he yelled, "Kordell, get in there and punt!" The late Michael Clarke Duncan, known for his role in the movie *The Green Mile*, was in the commercial, too.

✦ ✦ ✦

Even though the season hadn't started out too promising, we ended up making it to the playoffs for the sixth straight year. In doing so, Coach Cowher tied Hall of Fame coach Paul Brown for the most consecutive playoff appearances to start his career. And he did it with three different quarterbacks. Pretty impressive.

Our victory against the Patriots earned us a first-round bye and home field advantage when we faced the Pats again in the playoffs. We beat them 7–6 to advance to the AFC Championship—another opportunity to go to the Super Bowl.

I wanted to go to the Super Bowl so bad that year. It would've been my second Super Bowl appearance in my first three years as a Steeler. Unfortunately, we lost in the AFC Championship to John Elway and the Denver Broncos, who went on to win the Super Bowl.

Still, as I reflect on the season today, I can't look back on 1997 and *not* be thankful. The strides we made that year after so much transition were tremendously encouraging. To advance to the AFC Championship in my first year as a starting quarterback felt so good. It was pure joy and a huge accomplishment. It was everything I had worked toward—to be a quarterback in the NFL.

✦ ✦ ✦

As much fun as I had in 1997, my dad might have enjoyed the season even more. He attended almost every home game during the regular season in addition to the playoff games at Three Rivers. He didn't skip a beat. There wasn't a chance in the world he would miss having the opportunity to watch his son try to attain his dream. He was a proud father.

One thing he always—and I mean always—talked about was how beautiful Pittsburgh was. He loved the mountains and the hillside, and he loved how the seasons changed. Overall, I think visiting Pittsburgh and watching the Steelers in 1997 was a good escape for him. Whereas I had somewhat of an outlet—through football—to express myself after losing my sister the year before, I sometimes wondered if losing Terrance, his wife, and his only daughter—three immediate family members—ever cascaded down on him. Maybe watching me play football in 1997 helped him experience a sense of joy and freedom.

14

TOUGH DAY AT THREE RIVERS

I couldn't see myself anywhere other than Pittsburgh. First Slash. Then this. It was perfect. I loved the fans. I loved the culture. I loved our team.

I was full of hope, confident that I was special to Pittsburgh and Pittsburgh was special to me.

✦ ✦ ✦

In 1998, after coming so close the year before, I was dedicated to leading Steeler Nation to a Super Bowl.

We jumped to a 3–1 start, picking up right where we had left off the year before: a 20–13 win in Week 1 against Baltimore, a 17–12 win in Week 2 against Chicago, a 21–0 loss to Miami in Week 3, and then a 13–10 win against Seattle in Week 4. I wasn't playing especially great—I had six interceptions in the first three games, including three against Miami when they blew us out on the road, and only two touchdowns—but we were still winning.

In some ways, the start of the 1998 season went similarly to how 1997 had gone. A little rough. A little scary. But we were getting it done. As always. Once again, it wasn't pretty. Just like in 1997, we had Steeler Nation on the edge of their seats each game—partially, I'll admit, because of my inconsistent play. But all that mattered to me was that we were winning. And as long as I was quarterback, I had the confidence we could win. I might not have had the stats of other elite quarterbacks, but it felt like we won time after time after time.

After a bye in Week 5, we suffered a pretty big blow against former Steelers quarterback Neil O'Donnell and the Cincinnati Bengals in Week 6. Neil, a quarterback I've always looked up to, made some great plays down the stretch to steal the victory from us.

Personally, I had a decent game. In the wake of our star running back Jerome Bettis twisting his left knee, I rushed for over one hundred yards and had much of Pittsburgh talking about Slash again. Whenever they were talking about my diverse skill set, Slash, it was a good thing. Slash was a freestyle athlete, and when people saw a player who was as flamboyant as Slash transition into playing the vanilla, traditional quarterback position—you know, straight coffee, no cream, no sugar—well, I just think it was difficult for people to embrace him sometimes.

We responded to the heartbreaking loss to Cincy and won our next two games (we defeated Baltimore 16–6 and Kansas City 20–13), improving to 5–2 on the year. Just like in 1997, we were winning, and I had my sights set on one thing: a Super Bowl.

I'm not going to pretend that things were perfect in Pittsburgh at the start of the 1998 season. Having a new offensive coordinator in Ray Sherman was another transition that we had to work through in our offense; I especially struggled with it on a personal level.

The year before, I'd felt like Chan Gailey had allowed the offense to revolve around me—around my natural skill set and unique tendencies in my style of play. This involved both passing and rushing. Coach Gailey had confidence in me, which boosted my confidence in my abilities as a quarterback on the team. He had a lot of experience, having worked with John Elway and the Denver Broncos offense for several years, and I liked the way he went about things.

Our relationship had a rich history, too. He was the wide receivers coach for the Steelers from 1994 to 1996, so he knew my abilities and had already coached me by the time he became our offensive coordinator in 1997. He was my partner in crime, so to speak. When he went to the Dallas Cowboys in 1998, I felt like I lost someone who understood the way I played. Coach Gailey always talked about *what* was right, not *who* was right. That's why he saw players flourish.

Coach Gailey and I had something deep—much deeper than a typical coach-player connection. I kind of felt like he was my guardian angel in Pittsburgh. He was hard on me, but he was always in my corner. He was the person who really taught me the game of football on the professional level, from wide receiver to quarterback, and he allowed me to play aggressively. He knew my style, and he let me play it.

The offense felt entirely different in 1998 with Coach Cowher's hiring of Ray Sherman, who was a quarterbacks coach for the Minnesota Vikings before his arrival in Pittsburgh. It also seemed like we had a brand new offensive line and had lost a number of receivers.

In 1998, Coach Sherman was trying to do the best he could with what all the new talent we had. He was trying to figure it all out. God bless his soul, because he came into a tough situation, trying to get back to an AFC Championship and a possible Super Bowl. Any coach coming in at that time would have felt the pressure of cobbling together a new offense and getting us back to prominence.

Still, it was different. That season had a very different vibe than the year before, even if we started off with the same record.

✦ ✦ ✦

Week 9 changed the course of the season.

We entered the game with a 5–2 record, taking on the 3–4 Tennessee Oilers at Three Rivers Stadium. The Oilers hadn't won at Three Rivers since 1993, and we hadn't lost a regular season home game in ten games. Two quarters in, however, it looked like Tennessee would erase all of that; we entered halftime trailing 17–7.

Our 17–7 deficit wasn't really anything new. It wasn't something we weren't used to. The year before, it felt like all we did was come from behind, and in our five wins so far that year, we had only led at halftime in two. The year before, we won three games in overtime, and six of our twelve overall wins were by a touchdown or less.

We very rarely ran away with a win. But somehow, we always won.

Entering the second half, I was feeling good. We were at home, and even though trailing to the Oilers at home was kind of a humiliating thing, there was a sense that we were going to pull something out like we always did.

Tennessee tried to blow the game open with an unexpected onside kick to start the second half. Their sneak attack failed, and we gained possession at our own forty-one-yard line. I connected for a twenty-yard completion to Charles E. Johnson on the first play from scrimmage, and we ended up attempting a fifty-two-yard field goal. Norm Johnson missed, and the score remained 17–7.

The Oilers went three-and-out, and after a punt into our end zone, we took over at our own twenty with ten or so minutes left in the quarter. We started to march down the field; I completed two short passes to begin the drive. At this point in the game, I had completed fifteen of twenty passes with no interceptions, which isn't bad. We just struggled to score.

I really wanted to make something happen—no way did I want the Oilers to win their first game at Three Rivers in five years while I was the starting quarterback.

As we began our drive, I threw a pass to Charles up the field, and the pass was picked off—only my second interception in five games. I remember walking off the field, my frustration building. Tennessee ended up kicking a field goal to take a 20–7 lead.

There was a lot of time left, though—about eight or so minutes in the third quarter—and I completed my next three passes, again trying to make something happen. That's when I threw my second interception of the game.

When Tennessee took over, Eddie George had a big rushing play right up the middle for almost forty yards and a touchdown. Just like that, Tennessee had blown the game open and held a 27–7 lead. At the end of the third quarter, we turned the ball over on downs, and I could see the game starting to slip away.

Tennessee scored *again* at the start of the fourth to go up 34–7, but then we finally—*finally*—got into the end zone on our next drive. We marched about seventy yards down the field in two-and-a-half minutes. I went five-for-six on the drive, and we eventually scored on a short three-yard pass from me to Courtney Hawkins.

I completed a pass to Charles E. Johnson for the two-point conversion, and we trailed 34–15 with twelve minutes remaining in the game. I knew a comeback was improbable, but there was still a lot of time left, and I was starting to regain the confidence I'd had before I'd thrown two picks in the third quarter. Plus, a comeback had also been improbable the year before in our game against Baltimore on the road and in our Week 16 game against New England, and we'd come back then, didn't we? We always seemed to come back.

And I felt like we could do it again. Plus we'd made it look easy on the previous possession, scoring almost instantly.

Our defense forced Tennessee to go three-and-out. They punted, and we took over at our own twenty-four with a chance to make something magical happen.

The animosity in the stadium seemed to be building throughout the second half, but I have always felt that, in every challenge, an opportunity is presented to show your strengths. I was ready to show everyone that, no matter how ugly the game, I would lead them to victory.

I walked onto the field with new life and hope—hope that we could get it done. Again.

We were at our own twenty-four, and we lined up in the shotgun, as we had during the entire possession before. I took the snap, dropped back, didn't see anything, and threw a short pass to David Dunn.

Right when I threw it, my first thought was, *Crap.*

Picked.

Returned.

Touchdown.

Then came the boos bearing the full force of Steeler Nation.

I walked off the field to the sideline, ripped off my helmet, and said a number of things that shouldn't be printed. I looked up at the sky, the boos ringing in my ears. I was so angry. Angry at the throw. Angry at my performance. Angry at myself. I didn't take the boos personally. If you give fans a reason to boo, they will, and they should. As I've said before, it's only a *game.* This game, in particular, happened to be a terrible one for me.

But then, as my nightmare of a day continued, it got personal.

First, I was benched. Second, as I walked off the field and into the tunnel after our loss, someone threw a cup full of beer at my head that gushed into my eyes. I looked up. A man looked me dead in the eyes and yelled, "NIGGER!"

I continued walking, and my mind kept replaying what had happened. I couldn't believe someone would stoop so low as to throw a beer on me *and* call me what he did.

I hated opening myself up to a situation like that—to hostility between fans and players—but there was something about the incident that pushed me over the edge. I told the media that if it happened again, I was going to go into the freaking stands.

After the promise of 1997, the steady start to 1998, the normality of the first half against Tennessee, and the fact that I had been throwing the ball well until my three interceptions, it felt like my quarterbacking world had been flipped upside down.

15

RUMOR MILL

As I share some of the trials I experienced in Pittsburgh in the coming pages, I hope it is easy to see that I am being transparent out of respect for the reader. My intention is not to be dramatic or live in the past but rather to provide some of the raw emotion that I felt at the time.

Up until the 1998 season, I had experienced what most would consider to be a storybook career—from being surrounded by incredible talent at Colorado that allowed me to break offensive records left and right, to climbing so quickly on the draft board my senior season, to beginning my rookie season with the Steelers as a fourth-string quarterback and playing on the field midway through the season in my Slash role, to suddenly becoming the starting quarterback two years later. However, because the strife I experienced in Pittsburgh is often mentioned in discussions about my career, I think it would be an injustice to the reader to simply gloss over the hard times. Sure, I had some hard times, like anyone might experience in his or her profession, but I tried to work hard, have a good attitude, and care for people along the way. I also learned a lot about myself when it came to my commitment, drive, and determination in the game of football. I'm thankful for the trials because they made me into the person I am today and, in the end, strengthened me.

✦ ✦ ✦

It was a Tuesday when I got the call.

It was just a couple of days after our loss to the Oilers and the incident with the beer-throwing, name-calling fan. I was in my basement, watching the movie *The Thomas Crown Affair*, and my home phone rang. I found that strange for a couple of reasons: (1) I rarely got calls on my landline, and (2) it was late.

I decided I should pick up.

"Hello?" I said.

"Bro, you all right?" asked the person on the other end. I could tell that it was Dr. Frank Sessoms, a close family friend.

"Yeah, I'm fine," I said.

"You are?" he asked again.

"What are you doing calling me on my landline this late?" I laughed. "You know to call me on my cell."

He expressed to me that he had already tried calling my cell phone and that it was urgent.

"What the heck is going on?" I asked.

That's when Dr. Sessoms made me aware of a rumor he had heard that evening—that a Pittsburgh cop had supposedly arrested me in Schenley Park for performing lewd acts with a transvestite.

The rumor was so absurd it was almost funny. I dismissed it as barbershop talk. I had never been arrested or even pulled over by a cop for something as harmless as speeding in the city of Pittsburgh.

Every athlete deals with false rumors. It comes with the territory. And rumors always die because they are rumors. People aren't drawn to rumors; they are drawn to truth. Dr. Sessoms told me that he felt like he needed to call me because he cared about me and wanted to make me aware of what people were saying.

I assured him I was fine and went back to watching *The Thomas Crown Affair*.

✦ ✦ ✦

When I got to the Steelers facility the next morning, Teresa Varley, the fan club coordinator, asked me if I was doing all right.

By this point, I had completely forgotten about the phone call the night before. Why would it be on my mind? The story wasn't true, so I had dismissed it.

"I'm doing fine," I told her. "How about you?"

"Everything's pretty cool," she said, in kind of a weird way. "Um," she hesitated, "Mr. Rooney wants to see you."

"Wants to see *me*?" I questioned.

Mr. Rooney never wants to see me, I thought to myself.

"Yes," she affirmed.

I couldn't figure out why he wanted to meet with me. I knew it wasn't for any signing bonus. All I could think was that maybe it had to do with the loss on Sunday against the Oilers.

I walked into Mr. Dan Rooney's office and sat down. He was cool, calm, and collected, just like always. There isn't a pressure bone in his body. He's always just chilling.

"How ya doing, Mr. Rooney?" I asked nervously, wondering what was going on.

"Good," he said to me. "But how are *you* doing?"

The only thing I could think of that was kind of weighing on me was the loss on Sunday.

"I'm doing good, Mr. Rooney," I told him. "You know, just coming off Tennessee, man. People were throwing beer on me and stuff as I walked off the field."

"Try to recover from it, son," he said, in an understanding way. "Get ready for the next game. You're all right. You know, my dad had Terry Bradshaw as his quarterback, and I grew up seeing how they treated Terry. They called him dumb and said all kinds of stuff. Get ready for the next game, son."

"But *really*," he continued, "you sure you're doing all right?"

"Mr. Rooney," I said. "I'm doing fine."

"I know you're fine," he said. "But—"

"Mr. Rooney," I said again. "I'm doing fine. Nothing is wrong or anything. I just want to play."

He nodded, but he still seemed concerned.

"Why you asking me like that, Mr. Rooney?" I finally asked.

"You know," he said. "I was just making sure you're okay."

Remembering the rumor my buddy had called me about the night before, I finally realized what he must have been alluding to. I supposed that he probably had to meet with me to make sure that I hadn't been arrested and wasn't in trouble with the law.

"Is there anything that you have heard?" I asked.

"Well," he said. "You know I hear things all the time. And I just wanted to make sure you were fine."

"I want you to know that it's not true," I said.

"You don't have to explain it to me," he said. "Crazy things were said about Terry Bradshaw, too. Every quarterback that's come through here has dealt with it. And now you're the quarterback. So I just have to make sure you're doing fine."

"Mr. Rooney, I am one-hundred percent okay," I said. "One-hundred percent."

"Thanks, Kordell," he said. "Your coach also wants to see you."

◆ ◆ ◆

Coach Cowher was walking through the fire himself that year and dealing with his own batch of rumors. One rumor was that he was sleeping with his secretary. Another was that he was sleeping with my sister. Yes, my sister, who had passed away my rookie season. I was amazed how ignorant people could be to start a rumor like that. When you're not winning or you have an embarrassing loss, everything gets magnified. It seemed as if no one understood that better than Coach Cowher and me that season.

When I walked into his office, Coach Cowher had his head down. His eyelids looked a little heavy, his nose was red, and his eyes were all watery; it looked like he had been crying. He looked exhausted. I had never seen him look like that before. I wondered if it was allergies, not knowing if he had any, but I felt it probably wasn't.

"You all right, Coach?" I asked him.

"Yeah, kid," he said. "Just wanted to make sure you're doing good."

"I'm doing good," I said, getting to the point. "Is this about what Mr. Rooney just talked to me about?"

"Yeah," he said.

I told him the same thing I told Mr. Rooney—that it wasn't true. I was frustrated with the whole situation, especially in the context of the horrible week it had already been. I wasn't thinking about what people were talking about on the streets. I was thinking about my job. I was frustrated with the game we had just played. Upset that we lost. Upset that I got yanked. Upset that what I thought was a secure thing—my starting role—was now in question.

Now I had to deal with a ridiculous rumor. Arrested for performing lewd acts with a transvestite in Schenley Park? Seriously?

To clarify, I have no issues with people's sexuality, gay or straight, and I wouldn't have a problem with having a gay teammate. To each his own. That's not what bugged me about the rumor. What bugged me about the rumor was that it just wasn't true. Most people, I'd assume, would have a problem if things were being said about them that were not true.

Just like the beer and the n-word, the rumor was fabricated because someone was frustrated with my play on the field.

Since Mr. Rooney and Coach Cowher had both confronted me about the rumor, there was a good chance my teammates were talking about it as well. The team had bigger things to worry about—we were 5–3 and had just been embarrassed by the Oilers—but I knew I'd probably have to talk to them about this stupid rumor, too.

"Well, what do you want to do about this?" Coach Cowher eventually asked me.

"Coach, I don't know what to do," I told him. "What do you think I should do?"

"I think you should address the team," he said.

"Okay," I agreed.

✦ ✦ ✦

I had faced a serious rumor once before, back when I was at the University of Colorado, but it never really caught wind. It had to do with Coach McCartney's daughter.

His daughter had one child with Sal Aunese, a starting quarterback from Hawaii, and another child with defensive lineman Shannon Clavelle from New Orleans. My name got thrown into the mix for the most random of reasons. Sal was a quarterback like me, and Shannon was from New Orleans like me. Combine the two, and what do you have?

A quarterback from New Orleans.

Kordell Stewart.

This is how stuff gets started.

✦ ✦ ✦

I walked into our routine, early-morning meeting, and sat down next to Mike Tomczak and the other quarterbacks. Everyone was looking at me. Mike slapped me on the leg. "You good?" he asked.

"I'm all right," I said.

Coach Cowher walked in and started talking to the team. Next, he gave me the opportunity to address my teammates.

I stood up.

"Y'all know me," I told them. "Nothing happened last night, and I wasn't arrested. All I did was watch a movie."

I was twenty-six years old—just a young man playing football— and I had no idea how to handle something like that. I would have rather talked about football and moving on after a tough loss, being one of the leaders on the team. But instead I was forced to address my sexuality and the question at hand so they could see how absurd and farfetched the rumor was. I wanted them to understand very clearly that whoever started the rumor had to have been an ignorant fool.

16
ISLAND

By addressing the team, I thought I had extinguished the rumor. But it wasn't enough.

By noontime that day—the day I spoke to the team—Charles E. Johnson had received a phone call from our ex-teammate who played for the San Francisco 49ers all the way on the West Coast.

"What's up with your boy, man?" his friend asked, referring to me.

I couldn't believe it. In less than twenty-four hours, the rumor had traveled through the league, through the public, and across the entire country. And somehow, people believed it.

As the day ensued, the rumor continued to develop.

It came out that I supposedly went to jail.

It came out that I was seen in four or five different parks.

It came out that I paid my way out of the situation.

Anyone who is familiar with my story knows that the rumor followed me throughout the season and for the duration of my career.

All it did that season, however, was make me dig a little deeper. It made me plug into the Big Man Upstairs and rely on Him for strength through His Word. I read Proverbs. I read Psalms. I tried to gain wisdom that surpassed understanding. God knows I needed it. The Good Book helped me keep my eyes on the prize. It helped me use the situation I was in to make me a better player and a better person. All the negative energy that was put on me and the lies about who I was? I surrendered them to God. I asked Him to help me.

It made me discover joy and peace outside of the game of football and outside what people were saying about me. It made me find contentment within. At the end of the day, I was a child of God—and that mattered most. I wasn't defined by what people said about me; I was defined by what God said about me. I was defined by truth. I'm a

God-fearing man, and I decided that I would not disappoint the Man I worship and praise in how I reacted to the situation.

Out of selfishness, I might have felt like people were trying to shoot *me* down, but what they were really doing was shooting down God's creation—a man of joy and happiness who was just trying to enjoy the life God gave him. The rumor may have affected me to the point that it bothered me, but in the long run, it only made me dig deeper. It might have fazed me, but it did not break me. Truth be told, I do not believe in breaking points. I believe in having to *adjust*. I believe in *adapting*.

If the person who started the rumor ever reads this, I want to extend a warm and gracious "thank you"—because that rumor ultimately helped me grow and become the man I am today.

✦ ✦ ✦

The rumor made me better person in the long run, but my immediate reaction was to shell up and handle it on my own. In order to dig deep within me and figure out what I was made of, my most natural reaction was to isolate myself. I had to remove myself from the all the chatter and drama and enter a zone where I could focus on what was really important—football—and attempt to get the Steelers winning again. As I tried to press on amidst the lies, I naturally distanced myself from people.

Because the rumor never made sense to me, I didn't feel the need to continually acknowledge its existence. I *did* tell the media a couple times that it didn't happen; I just never had the grand stage to address it—because I didn't feel like I needed to. I was more concerned with keeping my job. I needed to stay the course and remain focused. I was a multi-talented player playing wide receiver, running back, quarterback, punter, and now I had this rumor? Compound that with being an African American quarterback whose style of play wasn't necessarily accepted in the NFL, and who was taking me seriously?

However, because I didn't really respond to the public on a grand scale about the rumor, I think people began to assume it was true. Because I kept somewhat silent—because I minded my own business—it was as if the general public assumed I was running from something. The rumor took on a life of its own, and my most natural reaction was to isolate myself more and more, living on my own little island just to stay strong and keep myself together.

Unfortunately, I do not think my isolation helped people's opinions of me. Though I was trying to handle the happenings of the season and the rumors maturely, I think my solitude resulted in people believing I was selfish—because I was quiet and seemingly unresponsive. The reality is that I was young and didn't know how to handle the situation.

✦ ✦ ✦

As I look back, that week alone changed Pittsburgh for me.

In 1997, the year before, I'd had all the respect a man could ask for; in 1998, however, it felt like there was a dark cloud of negative energy hovering over my head all the time. The rumor thickened the cloud.

All of a sudden, the dominant energy in Pittsburgh was doubt. The confidence and excitement that had surrounded the earlier years of my career seemed to have disappeared. In a week!

Not long after the rumor came out, I walked into a Pittsburgh restaurant with my girlfriend. Because I had a woman by my side, people in the establishment stood up and started clapping for us as the waiter took us to our table.

"What the heck is this?" I said to my girlfriend. "A circus?" I didn't know what to do so I clapped back and said, "Thank you."

It felt like people were watching me everywhere I went. Maybe it was just another glimpse of the spotlight. Whenever I hung out with anyone, I knew they were wondering if I was gay or straight. It was like a surveillance camera was on me at all times. People started looking at me and sizing me up. You can feel it when people are looking at you a little funny. I'm a quarterback. I see it all.

The rumor felt so much bigger than me—probably because it swarmed around the country and I started hearing it from every direction. Pittsburgh became a place of continual judgment, like my head was eternally on the chopping block.

The sad thing is that it all derived from the game of football. For someone to take the game of football—something I love to play— and turn it into something negative is wrong. For someone to take the football field—something that was my escape and my sanctuary when I lost my mother, when I lost my cousins, when I lost my sister—and turn it into something negative is disturbing.

I knew the only way to get my head off the chopping block, however, was to play better on the field—to turn the negativity into something positive. Consider Ben Roethlisberger, who became the Steelers quarterback in 2004. He had actual off-the-field legal woes, but after he won a Super Bowl, his reputation in Pittsburgh was restored.

The only cure, I figured, was to win. It was the only antidote that would silence the rumors and help my reputation—though I hadn't done anything to hinder my reputation to begin with.

It might have only been my second season as the starting quarterback for the Steelers, but I already knew one thing to be true: In Pittsburgh, winning cures everything.

17

SLUMP

The week following the release of the rumor, we were scheduled to play the Green Bay Packers on Monday Night Football.

I was ready to dominate. Football was my refuge.

Not friends.

Not teammates.

Not community.

My escape had always—*always*—been football.

After the week I'd had, an escape was exactly what I wanted and needed. I would find my vindication on the field.

Several articles leading up to the game concluded that our loss to the Oilers the week before might have been our worst loss in the Cowher era, and many members of the media had already labeled my season as a sophomore slump, as I'd thrown ten interceptions in eight games. It had been an abysmal season on *and* off the football field. Whatever 1997 was—the magic we made, the excitement in the city—1998 was the *exact* opposite. But there was still time, I figured, to turn things around and bury the off-the-field rumors by winning on the field.

I entered Monday night against Green Bay with something to prove.

After two straight completions, my third pass was a fifty-plus yard gain to Courtney Hawkins in single-coverage. Two plays later, I scrambled, bought some time, and found Charles E. Johnson wide open in the end zone for a touchdown.

That opening drive helped give me the confidence I needed to make a statement. I felt like myself in that game. Things were starting to feel normal and fun again.

On our second possession, I remember seeing Reggie White

burst through our line and dive at me. He grabbed my ankle, but I scrambled away and ran for thirty-some yards, until I was forced out of bounds inside the Packers' five-yard-line. I was so excited that I jumped higher than I've ever jumped before as I celebrated on the sideline. It was like all the energy bottled up from the entire week burst from my body.

Next, on the goal line, I made a mad leap over Packers nose tackle Gilbert Brown, who weighed 350 pounds, and scored our second touchdown, putting us up 14–0. It was still the first quarter. Nobody watching expected us to start like that, especially after our game the week before. We had only scored sixteen first-quarter points the entire season up until that game.

At halftime, we were leading 24–0.

We continued our dominance early in the second half, but Green Bay finally got on the board with a field goal late in the third quarter, giving us a 27–3 advantage entering the fourth quarter.

At the beginning of the fourth, we were on Green Bay's four-yard line, about to score another touchdown, when Coach Cowher decided to put Mike Tomczak in and line me up at wide receiver.

Mike snapped the ball. I ran my route and then looked at Mike for the throw.

That's when I saw Reggie White pummel him and force a fumble. Green Bay's Keith McKenzie scooped up the ball and had an open field in front of him. All ninety yards. Touchdown.

Then Brett Favre starting working his magic, leading Green Bay on a late-game comeback. Fortunately, they fell just short and we won 27–20.

Despite us nearly giving it away down the stretch, there were still a lot of positives to take from the game. We scored on our first five possessions and converted nine out of ten third downs before things turned sour. We came into the game emotionally charged from the week before, and we gave Steeler Nation something exciting to dwell on after a terrible, terrible week. A loss would have been a disaster; among other things, it would have been Coach Cowher's first time losing two home games in a row as our head coach.

For me, the game was a beautiful escape. It was a chance to disappear from reality—from the rumors, from the personal attacks, from people breathing down my neck about my performance.

The victory put us at 6–3 on the season and in a tight race for the Division. Despite the inconsistencies in our play, despite the rumors, and despite the simmering discontent among Steeler Nation, we were still in position to make the postseason. The season certainly felt worse than our record indicated. But we had life again, and I felt like my job was secure again. Winning was the best antidote for negativity, and it was a big win after such a negative week.

✦ ✦ ✦

The next week, we had an opportunity to get revenge against the Oilers, against whom I had thrown three picks just two weeks earlier. This time we were in Tennessee; like the week before, I was ready to go. It was another opportunity for redemption, this time against the team that had flat-out embarrassed us at Three Rivers.

It ended in a heartbreaking fashion.

We had a 14–13 lead in the fourth quarter, and a fourth-and-one opportunity on Tennessee's twenty-five-yard line with about four minutes left in the game; normally, Coach Cowher would have let the field goal unit come out to give us a four-point cushion, but since he didn't have confidence in our rookie, free agent kicker we had picked up that week because of an injury to our starter, he decided to go for it instead.

I got sacked, and Steve McNair and the Oilers marched down the field, kicking a field goal with six seconds left to take the lead. On the ensuing kickoff, we made a desperate attempt to work our way down the field with laterals and shenanigans, and we ended up fumbling. The Oilers rubbed salt in our wounds by scooping up the ball and scoring a touchdown, making the final score 23–14—nine of their points coming in the final six seconds of the game.

We hadn't been swept by the Oilers since 1993, when I'd been a junior at the University of Colorado. It was a really, really frustrating loss, and it was even more frustrating looking back on the entire season. We were 6–4, but two of those losses were games that we shouldn't have lost—the Cincinnati Bengals in Week 5 and the Tennessee Oilers in Week 11.

The difference between 1997 and 1998 was that in 1997, we were pulling out victories in close games—we were causing the heartbreaks. In 1998, however, it felt like teams were doing the exact same thing to us.

✦ ✦ ✦

The following game, I passed for over two hundred yards with no interceptions on our way to a 30–15 victory over the Jacksonville Jaguars at Three Rivers.

Our season might have felt like a train wreck four weeks before, but we made some repairs and got it back on the rails. Hines Ward, a rookie that season, was also really starting to mesh with the offense and was quickly becoming one of my primary receivers.

The rumors were still annoying. The pressure was still heavy. And I remained on my island trying to quarantine myself. But I knew a Super Bowl would free me from the nonsense. Once and for all.

✦ ✦ ✦

What happened at the beginning of overtime against the Lions on Thanksgiving is the perfect anecdote to describe the whole year.

Jerome Bettis and Carnell Lake, our two captains, ran onto the field for the coin toss. I was on the sideline, just trying to prepare and focus. I knew we needed the win or it'd be an uphill road for us to make the playoffs.

The referee that day was a man named Phil Luckett. In Pittsburgh, I bet they still forbid the mention of his name. I wasn't paying any mind to anything; it was just a standard coin toss.

Luckett flipped the coin. Jerome said, "Tails." Then Luckett said, "Heads is the call," as the coin landed on tails. Our bench erupted, realizing the referee had botched the most basic of things.

Jerome started freaking out, and Coach Cowher just kind of looked up at the sky, as if he didn't expect anything less from that season.

Nothing was a surprise anymore.

Oh yeah, and we lost the game. The Lions got the ball first, drove down the field, and kicked the game-winning field goal. In those days, before the overtime rule was changed in 2012, a field goal won the game in sudden death.

"What makes me mad," Coach Cowher told the media afterwards, "is that you fight and scratch for sixty minutes, and then it's decided by people wearing striped shirts. There's something wrong with that."

My teammate, linebacker Earl Holmes, said this to the media: "All I can say after this one is I've seen everything now."

That was 1998 for us.

✦ ✦ ✦

It was raining in Tampa Bay.

Trailing 6–3 in the third quarter in a must-win game—sitting 7–6 on the season—I threw another interception, my third pick in two games.

That's when Coach Cowher benched me.

As I watched Mike Tomczak play in my place, I became more and more frustrated. First, Mike fumbled, which led to a Tampa touchdown, putting them up 13–3. Then Mike threw a pick. When he threw the interception, I asked Coach Cowher, "So *this* is why you sit me on the bench? For *this*?"

"Yeah," he said. "I'm playing the guys that *want* to win."

"Are you kidding me?" I said. "You call a *fumble* and an *interception* winning?" I walked away—forcing myself to shut my mouth.

I felt like I had a will to win as much as anyone. "Giving up" was not in my vocabulary. Being *forced* to give up was worse. And being told I didn't care about winning was straight up insulting.

A storyline that eventually evolved from the game was the fact that I was crying on the sidelines after I got benched. Honestly, I did indeed have tears—not because my feelings were hurt—but because the game and the season meant so much to me, yet I was being contained on the sidelines.

After Mike's interception, Coach Cowher put me back in the game with 1:27 remaining, which was extremely confusing. By then, we were down 13–3, and it didn't matter. From that day forward, that's how Coach Cowher dealt with the quarterback position—with inconsistency and hesitancy.

Coach Cowher's doubts in me seemed to fuel the doubts of everyone else, adding gasoline to the fire. Though I always appreciated the opportunities Coach Cowher gave me—especially considering

I was a different style of quarterback—I sometimes disagreed with how he handled the starting quarterback position. This was one of those times. To be fair, emotions were also running extremely high at the end of the 1998 season, and many of us were acting out of our disappointment in different ways, searching for a solution.

It was a frustrating year to be a Steeler.

Throughout the entire 1998 season, I often flew out of Pittsburgh on Sunday after the game to be with my dad in New Orleans and then flew back on Tuesday. Pittsburgh hardly felt like home. When I attended the University of Colorado, I stayed there all summer. I hardly ever went home, except for on holidays. But in Pittsburgh, I had to get away. I needed to recover my peace of mind.

18

ORCHESTRA

The offseason heading into 1999 involved another transition in the hiring of a new offensive coordinator: Kevin Gilbride. I guess transitions are a norm in a league as competitive as the NFL, but for a quarterback, continually changing your offensive coordinator can be difficult. Chan Gailey left after the 1997 season; Ray Sherman was fired after the nightmare 1998 season; and Kevin Gilbride was hired in 1999. Three offensive coordinators in three years.

It's not really fair to place the blame for 1998 on Coach Sherman. I should take more of the blame than he should. Coach Sherman was asked to run an offense that took time to understand, and he was asked to do so during a season that felt like hell opened up. But perhaps Pittsburgh wasn't a good fit for Coach Sherman, and I was more than pleased with the hiring of Coach Gilbride in 1999.

In a lot of ways, Coach Gilbride and I needed each other. It was the perfect fit. We had both experienced frustrations the year before. Coach Gilbride—who had a reputation for mentoring some of the game's top passers like Houston's Warren Moon and Jacksonville's Mark Brunell—was fired six games into the San Diego Chargers' 1998 season for his inability to develop their first-round draft pick, Ryan Leaf. I needed Coach Gilbride like Coach Gilbride needed me. I wanted to get better, and I knew Coach Gilbride could help me. Coach Gilbride needed to win, and he needed me to help him do it. We were both looking to resurrect past success. And we were going to do it together.

Coach Gilbride studied my performances from the year before, and he concluded that most of the problems were in my head. He said I looked unsure of myself. He said I had lost the swagger I'd had my first three seasons in the NFL. He said I needed more mental preparation. He was trying to get me back on track again and narrow my focus.

The offseason heading into 1999 was really positive. I had time to myself—a sort of sabbatical—to escape from the drama and to work through the stresses of 1998. I tried to digest all of the emotions and events of 1998—the rumors about my sexuality, the poor play, the bad vibes—and put them behind me. I also went to Coach Gilbride's house in San Diego and hung out with him. Worked out with him. Spent time with him. What Coach Gilbride had done with Warren Moon was exciting to me, and I hoped we could do something similar in Pittsburgh.

I came back refreshed. I came back ready. It wasn't about any of 1998's circumstances or about anybody else. It was about going to work and getting things done. Period. From a mental standpoint, I tried to put myself in a good position to excel.

It seemed like Pittsburgh was putting me in position to excel as well. I had thought my future in Pittsburgh might be in question after 1998, considering we had lost our final five games of the season, causing Coach Cowher to miss the playoffs for the first time in his seven seasons with the Steelers; but the organization brought in Coach Gilbride to help me, signed me to a five-year extension, and drafted Louisiana Tech wide receiver Troy Edwards with the thirteenth pick in the draft. After everything that happened in 1998, I thought to myself, *A new contract? I'll take it.*

When you factored in Coach Gilbride, our additions on offense, the new contract, and all the subliminal things playing into my rejuvenated confidence, 1999 felt like coming out of a traffic jam onto an open road—a road of endless opportunity—leaving the clutter of 1998 far behind.

In short, however, 1999 turned out to be much like 1998.

Mike and I continued to play musical chairs at the quarterback position, my nightmares at Three Rivers continued (since the beer-and-n-word incident in 1998, I was 3–8 at Three Rivers as a starter; prior to that incident, I had been 10–1), and the offense that was trying to be implemented didn't seem to line up with our personnel. I learned a lot from Coach Gilbride, but his new run-and-shoot philosophies didn't seem to mesh well with the "Pittsburgh way." It didn't play to our strengths.

Things got so bad in 1999 that after we lost to Cincinnati in Week 12, falling to 5–6 on the year, Coach Cowher announced to the media after the game that I would return to playing my Slash role, and Mike would be the team's starting quarterback. I wouldn't play quarterback the remainder of the season. We lost the next three games, the longest Steeler losing streak since 1988.

It was apparent that the coaches were dead set on me not playing the rest of the season, because I wasn't even allowed to attend quarterback meetings. I hadn't been in receiver meetings since 1995!

All in all, we lost seven of our last eight games of the season to finish 6–10. Two years in a row without making the playoffs. Two years in a row of playing musical chairs at the quarterback position. Three years in a row of playing musical chairs at the offensive coordinator position.

And the orchestra would keep playing.

19

GOODBYE, PITTSBURGH

As I write about some of these difficult times within the organization and how confused I was during this time, I think it is easy to see how frustrated I was as a player. Yes, football is only a game, but it was also my profession and my life's passion. It was something that was close to my heart. More than that, I so desperately wanted to continue the Steelers' rich tradition and lead the organization (and Steeler Nation) to the Promised Land that it was sometimes agonizing to experience such a loss of control. I hope these raw emotions are relatable in this context, because we all experience frustrations in this life—and often these take place in our deepest passions. For me, that was football.

✦ ✦ ✦

Ever since I was benched in the nightmare game against the Oilers in 1998, I hadn't felt like I was truly the go-to quarterback for the Steelers. Though they might have named me the starter some weeks, the negativity, new offense, and chair shuffling made me feel like the coaches were constantly trying to find answers. Maybe the answer was right there in front of them all along.

The offseason heading into the 2000 season, Pittsburgh did not renew Mike Tomczak's contract; instead, the Steelers brought in a quarterback from the New York Giants named Kent Graham. As we went through training camp, OTAs, and practice, Kent looked phenomenal. But I was still No. 1 on the depth chart.

As the preseason ensued, I didn't even know that Kent and I were competing for the starting job. That's why I was surprised when Coach Gilbride told me the morning before our final preseason game that they were going to name Kent Graham the starting quarterback to kick off the regular season.

The decision came out of left field to me. Yes, Kent looked good in practice, but, as Allen Iverson says in his famous rant, "We talkin' about practice, we ain't talkin' about the game." (But, truth be told, Kent Graham was the best practice quarterback I had ever seen!)

I had a feeling that my starting quarterback days in Pittsburgh were over. Says my teammate Jerome Bettis in his book *The Bus: My Life In and Out of a Helmet*:

> *Coach Cowher and Kordell had kind of a love-hate relationship. For some reason, Coach would never really commit fully to Kordell. He committed to giving him a chance, a shot at the job, but he never gave him his full 100 percent, "You're-the-guy, let's go" endorsement. And because of that we had no consistent leadership from the quarterback position.*

> *I think if you would have taken a poll of the players, we would have voted for Kordell. Kordell was a friend, but I also thought he gave us the best chance to win ballgames. Graham was a guy who had lost starting jobs in Arizona and New York.*

> *Coach Cowher disagreed. Kordell became Coach Cowher's Plan B, which wasn't fair to Kordell or to the team. Kordell had split time with Tomczak in 1999 and now he had to watch as Graham took the job in 2000.*

I had been skeptical over the last year because of the musical chairs, so when they named Kent Graham as the starter before the season began, they confirmed my doubts.

The writing seemed to be on the wall. They were moving further and further away from including me in their future, which caused me to not have any feelings about the decisions being made in that organization.

◆ ◆ ◆

The year before, I had stayed on the field when I lost my starting job because I'd played receiver for Mike Tomczak. There would be none of that in 2000. Hines Ward, with two years under his belt, had developed into one of our primary receivers, and Troy Edwards, the Steelers' draft choice the previous year, was coming along as well. In the 2000 NFL Draft, the Steelers had also drafted Plaxico Burress with the eighth overall pick, so he had high expectations, too. I didn't want to play receiver, anyway. I was a quarterback. I did not feel like settling for anything less. In my mind, it was quarterback or bust.

However, I felt like I needed to stand by Kent and support him in his role as the starter. Though something very important to me—my football career—was not unfolding the way I wanted it to unfold, it wasn't worth accepting a victimized mentality. Though my specific role on the team had changed, my overall role had remained the same—to help the team win. This meant encouraging Kent and helping him become a better quarterback.

Along with trying to be there for Kent, I also began working harder than ever. Compassion and passion, baby. Treadmill. Lifting weights. Throwing the football after practice. Coming in on off days. Getting myself prepared just in case. I had always done that stuff, but I started doing it even more. Something about Kent being named the starter was very real to me. Five or six years into my professional career, it was obvious the Steelers were moving away from any future that had me in the blueprint. I had to do whatever I could to prove to them they were making the wrong move. And ultimately, I knew that my work ethic would influence Kent's, which would help the team win.

I remember our team psychologist Kevin Elko coming up to me one day while I was on the treadmill working out. "Man," he said, "you look focused. You look determined. I'm not going to ask you how you are doing because it's written all on your face. You're ready."

✦ ✦ ✦

We lost in Week 1. Then again in Week 2. And again in Week 3. Kent started all three games. And the coaches were planning on continuing to start him.

Truthfully, I saw things going south because there were too many players on the offense that didn't buy into the philosophy Coach Gilbride was trying to enforce with Kent at the helm. We were 0–3 to start the season for the first time since 1986. Combine Mike Tomczak's and Kent Graham's starts from the previous season, and we were 1–7. In our second season with Coach Gilbride trying to implement his run-and-shoot offense, it was becoming clearer and clearer that it wasn't working, no matter what quarterback he decided to use.

Kent hurt the bursa sac in his hip heading into our Week 4 game—just two days before our matchup against the Jags. I was named the starter for the game, but since Kent got hurt so late in the week, I hadn't taken any physical reps at quarterback with the starting group the entire week leading up to the game—only mental reps. I had spent the whole week playing quarterback on the scout team.

Truth is, if Kent hadn't busted his bursa sac that Friday, I'm confident I wouldn't have started a single game that season. The coaching staff was pretty set on Kent. Considering I'd been excluded from the quarterback meetings the year before, I was pretty convinced I either had one foot out the door or had already been kicked to the curb.

By this point, I had nothing to lose. In my mind, I was on my way out. I was determined to do whatever I could to help the team win. We were in a desperate state. After our first 0–3 start in fourteen years, it seemed quite possible that we were en route to our third straight season without making the playoffs—something that hadn't happened since the mid-'80s.

I remember walking off the practice field after practice on Friday, and Coach Cowher motioned for me to come over.

"Just play the game," he told me. "Don't worry about anything. Just be you."

I nodded.

"You hear me?" he said, looking me in the eyes.

"All right, Coach," I said.

Now it's time to play football, I thought to myself.

It was good he said that because it was about football, and that's what it is supposed to be about. And he wanted me to be myself.

Here comes the real Slim Shady.

And I stood up.

Few people expected us to beat Jacksonville in Week 4. The Jags had racked up the best record in our Division the year before, and we had never won in Alltel Stadium. But we won pretty handily 24–13.

There was a play that game, however, that seemed to accurately capture the situation I was in with the Steelers under Coach Gilbride and his desires to adopt the run-and-shoot offense.

I remember stepping up under center and noticing that the Jacksonville defense was in man-to-man coverage across the board. We were running a designed play for Plaxico; but once I snapped the ball, our offensive line and the oncoming rushers wrapped around me so much that the gates of heaven seemed to open in front of me. I couldn't see much because of the pressure and the push of the defense, but I saw the gaping hole in front of me, four offensive-linemen wide. So I tucked the ball and ran right up the middle—ten, twenty, thirty, almost forty yards.

We ended up scoring a field goal to take a 10–3 lead. When I was on the sideline following the drive, one of my teammates got my attention. "Coach Gilbride wants to talk to you," he said.

I picked up the phone to talk to Coach Gilbride, still high-fiving my teammates as they came up.

"Why the *f&%$* are you running?" his voice blared through the phone. Apparently, he was angry at me for running for a first down instead of throwing the ball downfield to Plaxico.

"I couldn't see Plaxico," I said. "I couldn't see nothin'."

I was shocked he was yelling at me, but at the same time I wasn't really shocked at all.

"Why the *f&%$* are you running?" he asked me again.

"But we got a first down," I said. Because I had a game to focus on, I didn't have time for confrontation, so I said I had to go and hung up the phone.

Dick Hoak, the running backs coach, then called down to the field and said to me, "Don't worry about that, Kordell," said. "You let that go. You're playing the game the way you know how to play the game. You're doing a great job, kid. Keep playing."

Did Coach Gilbride want the Steelers to excel, or did he just want his system to work?

After that, I adopted an "I don't give a damn" mentality when it came to Coach Gilbride. The run-and-shoot style offense was not working in Pittsburgh. I was going to be who I was and let the chips fall where they may.

Offensively, that entire game against Jacksonville felt like old times again—with Jerome and me doing our thing and perfecting the rushing game, going for nearly 215 yards combined.

Truth is, Jerome's role never should have been to sit on the bus and watch; his role was to *be* the Bus and run over the opposing defense. As for me, why not allow my unique abilities as Slash to flourish? Can I get an "amen"?

It was time to go back to doing things the "Old Pittsburgh Way." The way it should have always been.

✦ ✦ ✦

Following Jacksonville, Coach Cowher said I played a great game and made wise decisions, but he also said Kent would still be the starting quarterback when his hip felt better. In Pittsburgh, we had a rule: Starters don't lose their jobs to injuries. I understood.

Kent's hip wasn't better in time for our Week 5 game against the undefeated New York Jets, however, so I was once again named the starting quarterback. It was another game that hardly anyone expected us to win. Once again, we were on the road. And once again, we were facing a top team, this time one that was off to a 4–0 start.

We won.

Again.

Handily.

We defeated the Jets 20–3; Jerome and I combined for almost 150 yards of rushing, and I had another game without an interception. We had been expected to lose those two games on the road, but we had counted two victories. I had been given a job to do, and it felt good to get it done.

Kent's three straight losses and my two consecutive victories made the next week hell for Coach Cowher. After our victory against the Jets, however, Coach made it very clear to the media that Kent would be the starter against the Cincinnati Bengals at Three Rivers Stadium in Week 6, and he stuck by his decision throughout the week.

All I could to was perform in whatever role I was given to the best of my ability. It's true that I might not have always agreed with the decisions that were made in Pittsburgh, but it wasn't ever worth wasting energy and emotion over something that I could not control. I was working hard, giving my all, and that was all I could do. I was happy we could win a couple games after losing our first three.

✦ ✦ ✦

The middle of the 2000 season became the same old story it had been for the previous two seasons at the quarterback position: musical chairs.

Kent started against Cincinnati at home, and I didn't play; we won 15–0 in our third straight victory. Kent started against Cleveland at home and struggled, and I finished the game; we won 22–0 for our fourth straight victory. I was given the starting role against Baltimore on the road, and Kent didn't play. We won 9–6 for our fifth straight victory. Once again, it seemed, I had disproved Coach Cowher and Coach Gilbride's quarterback "solutions."

We were 3–0 in games I had started that year, thus earning me the starting quarterback position once again. We lost our next game against Tennessee by two points, the following game against Philadelphia in overtime by three points, and the next game against Jacksonville by ten. We then defeated Cincinnati 48–28 to improve to 6–6 on the season.

✦ ✦ ✦

I was given the nod to start at home against Oakland on December 4.

We marched right down the field on our opening drive, and I threw a nineteen-yard touchdown pass to Bobby Shaw to give us a 7–0 lead.

Unfortunately, I hyperextended my knee at the end of the first quarter and had to come out of the game. Walking back to the locker room, my mind swirled as I asked myself, "What can I do? What can I do?" We had started the game off so well. I wanted to keep playing.

I went to the equipment room and started watching the game on television. We had fallen behind 17–7. Determined to do something, I walked from the equipment room to the trainer's room and told our trainer John Norwig, "I need to get taped."

"If you want to go back out there, let's do it," he said. "But what I saw happen to your knee was bad. Whatever your decision is, let's go."

It hurt to walk, but John Norwig did one heck of a job taping it, wrapping it so I wouldn't be able to bend it and hyperextend it again while I was playing.

As I was getting it taped up at halftime, Bobby Shaw came up and asked me, "What's up man? You coming back in?" Wayne Gandy came up to me and said, "What's the deal, bro?" Jerome came up to me and started talking about his thumbs and knees being taped, and Courtney mentioned something about his knee. They were making sure that I understood that everyone was hurt and that they really *needed* me to play hurt as well. The fact that so many of my teammates wanted me to get back in validated my decision to risk it, get taped, and go back in.

I told my teammates, "I'm going back in."

Everyone was amped up.

And so began our comeback.

We came right out and marched down the field. I completed six of eight passes, and I threw a touchdown pass to Mark Bruener to bring the score to 17–14. We faced the same deficit entering the fourth quarter.

At the start of the fourth, I broke free on a quarterback draw for a seventeen-yard touchdown run, making the score 21–17, which ended up being the game-winning touchdown for our 21–20 victory over the best team in the AFC.

After I scored, Hines Ward and Mark Bruener jumped on me and celebrated. After starting the game so strong and being down 17–7 at halftime and then coming back to the game and scoring two touchdowns, my emotions were flying.

Some in the media said it was the gutsiest and best performance of my career. Some said it was "Terry Bradshaw like."

There had been a lot of negativity up to that point, but our comeback win against Oakland and the fashion in which we did it seemed to change everything. I might have gotten sent to receivers' meetings the year before and been benched for Kent Graham at the start of the year, but I showed the Steelers I still had what it took to the lead the team. All I needed was the chance.

Remember, all the quarterback drama had been confusing and frustrating for my teammates, too. Not just me. The musical chairs left them just as aggravated as I was because there was no consistency. How do you get players on offense to play to their full potential when nothing is steady?

The game was a big moment for me, for the city, and most importantly, for my teammates because it helped them realize who their quarterback was.

I started the remainder of the year, but our difficult start to the season proved to be too big of a mountain climb. After a 0–3 start, we finished 9–7 (our first winning season since 1997), but we failed to make the playoffs for the third straight year. Reflecting on the 2000 season, Jerome says this in his book:

> We won seven of the eleven games he (Kordell) started, including four of the last five. But the move came a little too late.
>
> Part of the blame has to go to Coach Cowher. I'm not sure he ever knew what to do with Kordell. Kordell was an unusual talent, like a Michael Vick, a Donovan McNabb, or a Randall Cunningham. I think if you asked Coach Cowher now if he made some mistakes with the way he handled Kordell, he would say he did. Sadly, I think it affected Kordell's development of a quarterback.
>
> Had we made the playoffs—the Colts got the last spot in the AFC—I dare say we would have reached the AFC Championship. We had that good of a football team by the end of December. Kordell had earned our confidence.

✦ ✦ ✦

During those two seasons under Coach Gilbride, I tried to approach the game with an "it is what it is" attitude. Our personalities and different approaches to the game might have clashed, but he was still my coach. There was nothing I could change. He was still the figure in authority, and as long as he was my coach, my role as a player was to listen to him and try to apply the things he told me.

Though a career in the National Football League is often approached with a results-driven attitude, one of the things I always found to be true—whether I was happy or frustrated, whether we were winning or losing—was the reality that I could learn something in the situation I was in. In fact, I think I learned even more about myself in the down years. When it's all said and done, adversity is all about how you handle it. For the most part, I felt like I handled things okay in Pittsburgh considering the circumstances. Difficult situations can help you become a better person if you allow them to mold you—if you approach the situation with a glass-half-full mentality.

During those down years, my father would sometimes call and ask me, "You need me to come up there, son?" I know he could tell I was discouraged.

In the first three years, I'd simply been playing a game I loved; now I was forced to maturely handle the lies and rumors and all the drama associated with playing quarterback for the Pittsburgh Steelers. Consequently, I was forced to grow up quicker. Ultimately, I am thankful for this.

Because football was an outlet for me in a world that entailed a lot of personal loss, I sometimes took things personally when I felt like something was unfair—like a rumor that wasn't true or the decision-making of certain coaches. But in the end I'm thankful for all these things because I grew as a person in ways that went far beyond a game. Trials ultimately helped strengthen my character, integrity, drive, and work ethic.

There's no doubt, however, that by the conclusion of the 2000 season, I felt like it was time for a change. I never thought I would feel that way. Pittsburgh was all I knew at the time. It was where I started. I had wanted to be a Pittsburgh Steeler for my entire career, especially after those first three seasons. But it reached a point at which I felt like I had to get out of there; it all came to a climax in 2000.

As inconsistent as the coaches had been, I wondered what the

2001 season would be like. I couldn't keep going back and forth from the bench to the field. I couldn't keep feeling like I was going to get taken out if I made one bad play. The musical chairs didn't work in 1998, when I first started being questioned and Mike got some playing time. It didn't work in 1999, when Mike got most of the starts. And it didn't work in 2000, when Kent Graham was starting at the beginning of the season.

I needed a change of scenery. I was tired. Part of me would have loved to go to Miami and be around Chan Gailey, who was their offensive coordinator at the time, or move to a different situation where I could be myself again. I was thankful for how Pittsburgh had given me a chance and a once-in-a-lifetime opportunity for the first three years of my career, and I was even grateful that the ensuing challenges had propelled me into an area of personal, spiritual, and emotional growth—but at the same time, I hoped I could start anew.

20

COMEBACK SONG

After three years of negativity but finally showing signs of life in 2000, it was mandatory that Coach Cowher and I have a conversation. We needed clarity about the past and a better understanding of the present, and, most importantly, we needed to move into the future—whatever that meant.

The 2000 offseason was a crossroads for me to decide whether or not I wanted to go back to Pittsburgh. That decision was up in the air.

Coach Cowher called me when I was at my new home in Atlanta, and for the first time, I communicated my concerns to him. I told him I didn't appreciate how he didn't stick with me when times got tough in Pittsburgh and that I wasn't sure whether or not I wanted to return to that mess. He listened to me and allowed me to get everything off my chest, which I appreciated.

That offseason, I disappeared from Pittsburgh. I needed to debrief.

I wanted Coach Cowher and the franchise to have what they wanted. And if they didn't see me in their plans, I didn't want to hold them back.

"Coach, I just want to make it right," I remember telling him over the phone. "I want to make this good. I want to make this right. It doesn't have to be this hard." It was my last plea, because I truly wasn't planning on coming back. That was the last thing I wanted to do.

Dad knew I needed leave, too. He had seen me stressed for three straight seasons and hated seeing me like that. He finally told me, "Do what you have to do to make you happy," implying that my current situation wasn't the answer. That was tough to hear. It was tough because I knew the truth—that I wasn't happy there—and that off-season, I finally began to accept it.

✦ ✦ ✦

Between 1998 and 2000, I felt like I was dissecting my game more than ever before, and this made me more insecure about my game than ever before. I began thinking to myself on a continual basis, "Am I really *this* bad?" It was as if every time I walked off the field, I was nitpicking about hypotheticals in my head:

I put it on the back number, and I could have put it on the front number.

If I'd stepped a little bit more at 4 o'clock as opposed to 3 o'clock, maybe the handoff would have been a little cleaner.

If I had called a snap count on two, maybe it would have worked and I could have gotten them offsides.

Those were seriously the kinds of super-specific hypotheticals I agonized about. I was trying hard to find answers. Real hard. But I couldn't.

It was difficult because I'm a competitor—to the point where sometimes I blame myself so I can get better. But by this time, I didn't know what to blame myself for anymore. I had nothing left. I was out of blame. The blame tank was empty! I had no credit card to swipe to put some blame gas back in the blame tank!

That offseason, I started praying, "Big Man, I'm tired. I want to talk to You for a little while." Again, I read from the Psalms and Proverbs every day. Revisiting them helped keep me disciplined. Psalm 23 ("The LORD is my shepherd, I lack nothing. He makes me lie down in green pastures . . .") meant something different every time I read it. The Good Book gave me something to chew on and think about every single day. I may not have gotten an immediate answer to my prayers, but by the end of each day, I had more and more clarity.

All in all, I took comfort in knowing the Big Man Upstairs is consistent. He's always there. He has all the answers. Eventually I stopped asking why Pittsburgh was such a struggle and instead just asked God for understanding and for peace. What God gave me got me to a place that allowed me to be comfortable. Reading the Word helped me realize that it wasn't about anyone else. It wasn't about what people were saying. It wasn't about how people were acting. It wasn't about what people didn't understand. It wasn't about them or the rumor or the musical chairs. Beyond all the negative and draining energy that seemed to drag me down, which could easily and consistently take me away from football, there was a much greater story.

✦ ✦ ✦

As the offseason unfolded, a couple of key components clicked into place.

First, Coach Cowher hired the tight ends coach Mike Mularkey as the new offensive coordinator and Tom Clements as Pittsburgh's first-ever quarterbacks coach.

I had always liked Coach Mularkey. He had been the tight ends coach in Tampa for a couple of seasons before becoming the Steelers' tight ends coach in 1996. During his first two years in Pittsburgh, he worked alongside Chan Gailey. He had seen me endure everything in that city, from the highs of 1996 and 1997 to the lows of 1998, 1999, and 2000. I felt like he understood my style on the field and my personality off the field, because he had been around me for so long. Coach Clements had also been a quarterbacks coach for the Kansas City Chiefs and the New Orleans Saints and for Notre Dame at the college level.

I came to like Coach Mularkey even more that offseason. He actually traveled to my home in Atlanta to reach out to me while I was avoiding Pittsburgh. We played golf at the Golf Club of Georgia, and he talked to me in a very non-confrontational way. He wasn't pushing me to come back; he had no ulterior motive. He just let me in on his vision and what he wanted to do with the offense in the 2001 season. He took it on himself to come to Atlanta and spend some time trying to help me understand that I was the quarterback.

"This will be *your* offense," he told me. "You can go out and make the most of it."

The offense he talked about was the exact opposite of Coach Gilbride's and was much more in line with Coach Gailey's. It wasn't so structured. It gave me more freedom. It was all about the game coming to me, not me trying to control the game. The way he talked actually got me excited about the possibility of returning. Those two years under Coach Gilbride had felt like ten.

That offseason, some complained about my invisibility. I wasn't showing my face in Pittsburgh, nor did I have a desire to show my face in Steel City. I wasn't responding to interview requests. I wasn't attending any events in Pittsburgh. I was minding my own business. It was a crossroads for me concerning my future as a Steeler. Some in the media said I was running from the drama—from the city. But I just wanted to play football. With Coach Mularkey, it sounded like I would be able to do just that: play football.

He was the sole reason I decided to return. One hundred percent. No doubt about it. Taking some time off and talking to Mike Mularkey gave me the clarity I needed to return. It was time for me to put my work boots on, see it through, and return to Pittsburgh. I was excited to play football again.

For the first time in a long time.

21
BACK TO BEING ME

By the time I returned to Pittsburgh, I had mentally emptied myself of my preconceptions. My father had told me in the offseason, "If you go back or when you go back, you have to go back and make it work; you can't enter the season with doubt." Throughout everything, my dad was always a beacon of perspective, encouragement, and hope. He was my rock.

And so it was decided: I was going to be *me*. No coach was going to turn me into something I wasn't, and no rumor was going to make me shell up into something I wasn't. Benching me couldn't run me out of town, and neither could micromanaging the way I played a game I loved. Dumping beer in my eyes wasn't going to make me go away. I was determined not to let any person or any circumstance take up negative space in my head. I told the media it'd take a straitjacket and a ship to Hong Kong to make me leave. I was determined to see it through.

◆ ◆ ◆

The 2001 season was also our first year playing at Heinz Field. Our days at Three Rivers Stadium were over. Heading into the 2001 season, everything felt new and good and right, down to the last detail—a new offensive coordinator, a new quarterbacks coach, and even a new stadium.

Our first game of the season, however—after a strong finish the year before and a positive preseason that gave Steeler Nation a glimpse of Coach Mularkey's vision for the offense—was a dud.

Everything about that game was dark and gloomy, including the weather. All day, the tropical Jacksonville climate went back and forth between downpours and extreme humidity. I sprained both my ankles in the game. We lost 21–3, and the rain apparently affected us, as we dropped a number of snaps and passes. I had two interceptions. It was the furthest thing possible from the declaration of a new era and offense.

✦ ✦ ✦

Two days after losing our opener to Jacksonville, our three-year slump and our woes became the last thing on our minds. That's because of the tragedy that transpired on September 11, 2011—when the twin towers of the World Trade Center fell and shook the entire nation.

The focus became much bigger than a football game. Football suddenly seemed so petty, so small. People were dying. Our nation had been attacked. Our football problems seemed to vanish as we grieved along with the rest of our devastated country.

We didn't play another game until three weeks later, on September 30.

✦ ✦ ✦

When we played the Buffalo Bills three weeks later, many of us were teary-eyed and moved during the pregame tribute to America. The governor of New York, George Pataki, gave a speech before the game. Being in New York made it especially powerful; more than one hundred firefighters, police, and other civil servants who had helped with the rescue at Ground Zero gathered on the field for the special tribute.

It felt weird, honestly, to be playing a *game* in the wake of a national tragedy. But at the same time, one of my favorite things about football is that it is an avenue to joy and an escape to those watching. Maybe in some way, taking the field to play a football game could help our nation move on by returning to a state of normalcy.

We ended up defeating the Buffalo Bills 20–3, but our offense was just as bad as the week before. It wasn't a good start for me—the media called me "miserable" that week—and it was an even worse start for Coach Mularkey. I completed just over one hundred yards of passing, and I underthrew a number of throws.

But we won—our first victory in Buffalo in twenty-three years and our first win of the season.

✦ ✦ ✦

By our third game of the season against Cincinnati, our offense finally started making some progress. I connected on passes. Jerome rushed for more than 150 yards. And Coach Mularkey's play calling—the quarterback draws, the quick pitches, the plays that aligned with my strengths—was praised by the media following our 16–7 victory over the Cincinnati Bengals.

It was also our first game at Heinz Field—our home opener coming six weeks into the season because the September 11 terrorist attacks had caused many games to be postponed. The biggest storyline of that game, however, was Jerome. Not only did he have a stellar game, but he also became the fourteenth player in the history of the NFL to rush for ten thousand yards. That was special.

We were 2–1, and our offense was showing signs of life.

Coach Cowher called them baby strides.

✦ ✦ ✦

We made bigger strides the following week, defeating Kansas City 20–17 on the road to take first place in our division for the first time in three years. Three long, painful years. We may have started 1998 with a 3–1 record and 1999 with a 2–0 record, but those seasons quickly spiraled out of control. This was the first time since 1997 that we began to finally feel like the Pittsburgh Steelers: a franchise that wins and a franchise that runs the ball.

I was also starting to feel confident in our game plan for the first time in a long while. I felt more like myself. All of this goes back to Coach Mularkey—he ultimately saved the day. He gave me the green light and helped me understand that the offense was mine. My performance, he said, would determined how far we went that season. And he handed me the keys.

✦ ✦ ✦

We defeated Tampa Bay on the road 17–10, bringing our record to 4–1.

Five games into the season, I was averaging nearly thirty-five rushing yards per game. We were running rollouts and bootlegs, and Jerome's and my combined rushing made us the NFL's top rushing team. Back to the old Pittsburgh way. Grinding it out on the ground. Methodical and effective.

Then, in our sixth game of the year, on Monday Night Football in front of a home crowd, we beat a team that had defeated us seven straight times: the Tennessee Titans, the reigning AFC Central Division champions.

I passed for over 230 yards; Plaxico had over 150 receiving yards and was our first receiver to catch for over 100 yards in a game since 1999; Jerome had a couple of touchdowns; and Coach Cowher even called a play to run a fake field goal with Kris Brown that resulted in a first down. Coach always had something up his sleeve for Monday Night Football. We even ran a play that game in which Hines Ward took a direct snap while I was on the sideline; he ran for almost forty yards, and the crowd went berserk. Everything was working. Steeler Nation was excited again.

We were 5–1.

✦ ✦ ✦

At one point during our five-game winning streak, I remember being with my teammates in the huddle at the end of the game. We were winning—on the brink of securing the victory—and I heard Coach Cowher yelling from the sideline.

"Kordell!" he screamed. "Kordell! Kordell!"

He was obviously trying to get my attention.

"Don't look at the sideline, y'all," I said to the guys in the huddle.

"Kordell! Kordell! I know you can hear me!" he kept yelling.

Yes, I did hear him, but I chose not to acknowledge him. I wanted to stay in the moment with my teammates. I already had everything I needed from Tommy Clements in order to run the next play, and I didn't see the point in having a conversation with Coach Cowher while I was on the field. I had two coaches I could talk to—Coach Clements and Coach Mularkey; I figured I could talk to Coach Cowher at another time. Looking back, it was as if I became so immune to the ebb and flow of emotions during the "musical chairs" period that I became emotionless in 2001. I didn't want to leave that moment on the field.

Once the game was over, I went over to Coach Cowher. "Coach, I heard you call. What did you want?" (I tried to come across as all innocent.)

"It's too late now," he said. "We won."

Yep, I said to myself. *That's what I thought.*

I'm not sure if Coach Cowher even remembers this instance, but the only reason I share it is because I think it reveals the "my way or the highway" attitude I carried throughout the 2001 season. I am not saying this was the most mature mindset, but I think it demonstrates how desperately I wanted to win and how I didn't want to be distracted.

Coming off our five-game winning streak, we probably should have improved to 6–1 the following week, but instead we lost 13–10 to Baltimore—our first loss at Heinz Field that season. Kris missed four field goals, three of which went wide right. I felt terrible for him, especially when our fans started booing him.

I had been there. I had felt that. It's not fun.

We were 5–2.

The next week on the road against Cleveland, we bounced back, winning 15–12 in overtime. Our kicker Kris also made a comeback, making five of six field goals.

However, he missed arguably the most important field goal of the game, a forty-five-yard attempt at the end of regulation that would have won us the game. The only reason I bring this up is because I knew, right when he missed it, that it would be the only kick that would be remembered.

Kris responded well in overtime, however. I remember Jerome coming up to him on the bench once we had won the coin toss.

"I'm going to give you another chance," Jerome told him.

Lo and behold, Jerome had nearly a thirty-yard carry on the first play of overtime and logged around fifty total rushing yards in that overtime period. We—or Jerome, rather—coasted down the field and set Kris up for another field goal, which he made, bringing us to 6–2 on the season.

But Kris's redemptive accuracy and game-winning field goal in overtime weren't enough to earn his salvation among Steeler fans. At our next home game, a 20–7 victory against Jacksonville, the Heinz Field crowd booed him whenever he took the field.

The last time they had seen him, he had missed four field goals on his home turf. Of course, he had nailed five of six (including a game-winning field goal) the week before on the road, but that was irrelevant to them. I could see Kris feeling the same pressure at Heinz Field that I had felt at Three Rivers for several years.

As we approached halftime, our field goal unit took the field, and the fans started booing Kris once again. I felt terrible for him, so I ran out onto the numbers, put my hands in the air, and started trying to hush the crowd. Since I was having a good year, Pittsburgh liked me again; and since they liked me again, they started listening to me again—first growing quiet and then starting to cheer for Kris. That's right, *cheering*. From boos to cheers in a matter of seconds—the only thing that isn't fickle about Steeler Nation is their passion.

Kris made the field goal at the end of the half. He was two-for-two that game with a forty-eight-yarder and a twenty-eight-yarder. We defeated Jacksonville 20–7 and improved to 7–2.

Kris, for the record, was one heck of a kicker.

We defeated the Titans 34–24, our first victory in Tennessee since the Titans had moved from Houston to Nashville in 1997. The following week, Jerome got injured in our 21–16 victory at home against Minnesota. Though we were 9–2, Jerome's injury seemed to stop our season in its place.

The overall feeling in Pittsburgh was "Bettis or Bust"; in other words, people felt that if he went down, so would we. There were a number of factors to our success that year, but Jerome was undoubtedly the glue that held everything together. So when he re-injured his hip—which had been bothering him the previous week—I think much of Pittsburgh expected the season to venture into a steady decline.

That Monday, the news wasn't about how we had just won our fourth game in a row or how we had won nine of our last ten games. The stories were all about Jerome, and understandably so. Right when our team had seemingly broken free from our three-year drought— when we were once again winning and had become so unstoppable that the prospect of a Super Bowl didn't seem like such a far-fetched idea—the key to our success went down. Jerome ended up remaining sidelined for the rest of the regular season and into the playoffs.

Pittsburgh Post-Gazette columnist Ron Cook wrote:

> *The Steelers know.*
> *They go as Bettis goes.*
>
> *Never was that more obvious than after Bettis limped off late in the third quarter yesterday of what ended up as a lucky 21–16 win against the Minnesota Vikings.*
>
> *You and the Steelers are starting to think about the Super Bowl now that they're 9–2 and have the best record in the AFC?*
>
> *Bettis had better stay healthy.*
>
> *That's no knock on Chris Fuamatu-Ma'afala, who had 11 mostly fruitless, fourth-quarter carries before finally breaking off a 46-yard run to ice the victory. It's no knock of Amos Zereoue, who's limited to spot duty because of a separated shoulder.*
>
> *They just aren't Bettis.*
> *Few, if any, NFL running backs are.*

Whereas this was the mood in the city, I was not discouraged. Of course, I hated that one of my best friends in Pittsburgh and the best player on our team was hurt. But I now felt like the responsibility was mine, and all the pressure was on me to get it done—which was actually a comfortable feeling. For the first time in my career, I felt like this was my time. In the wake of Jerome's injury, there was a switch in responsibility. It was the first time since college that I felt like the organization and coaching staff needed to depend on me.

✦ ✦ ✦

In our next game against the 7–4 Jets, Hines and I teamed up for ten completions for 124 yards. I had my fifth two-hundred-yard passing game of the season, and Hines had a career high in receiving yards. Kris continued to struggle at Heinz Field, missing another pair of field goals—but it didn't matter. Jerome was sidelined—but it didn't matter.

We won—*again*—defeating the Jets 18–7.

It was our fifth win a row, putting us at 10–2 on the season.

✦ ✦ ✦

The game before had been all about Hines and me. The next week against Baltimore was about Plaxico and me. I passed for 333 yards, a career high for me, and Plaxico had 164 yards on eight catches, a career high for him. We won 26–21, our sixth victory in a row and second in a row without Jerome.

It was an especially fulfilling victory as it was against Baltimore, the defending Super Bowl champions. We despised Baltimore. They had been trash-talking us all week since they had already beaten us once that year, and Ravens tight end Shannon Sharpe tried to get in Plaxico's head by badmouthing him days before the game. So what did we do? We both went out and had career highs. The victory also secured our fifteenth AFC Central Division title and an automatic playoff berth, our first berth in three seasons.

Our record now stood at 11–2—the best in the AFC.

✦ ✦ ✦

The following week, we put on another clinic in front of our home crowd and beat Detroit 47–14, which earned us home field advantage in the playoffs. It was our seventh win in a row and third without Jerome.

We were 12–2.

All throughout 2001, we were playing with a real sense of freedom. As strange as this might sound, I think the seriousness of the 9/11 terrorist attacks made everyone appreciate the game of football a little bit more—because we approached that entire season with perspective. Football became a *game* again. It became enjoyable again. There were crises in the world far more serious than the simple game of football. And yet, football was an opportunity for Americans to come together and momentarily remove themselves from the turmoil the nation was experiencing.

✦ ✦ ✦

My father came to every single home game my 2001 season. I think what he enjoyed most about watching me was that, for the first time in several years, he got to see me enjoying myself. He got to see me play the quarterback position the way I knew how to play it.

What an amazing season it was! The trust was there. The willingness for input was there. It was as if the handcuffs had been removed from my wrists. It seemed like the coaching staff had realized everything that had gone wrong the previous three seasons and had suddenly started doing exactly the opposite. Coach Clements, who fully saw my talents and abilities, and Coach Mularkey, who built our offense around our strengths and the personnel we had, seemed to be the difference makers that season.

Overall, it was a joyful year. In Pittsburgh, as odd as it sounds, the mood of the city was determined not just by wins and losses but also by how we won and how we lost. In 2001, it felt like all we did was win. And therefore, the city was upbeat.

✦ ✦ ✦

We still didn't have Jerome for our next game on the road against the 4–10 Cincinnati Bengals on New Year's Day. It was the fourth game in a row he had missed, which was really something, considering he had only missed three games in nine seasons.

The game started the same way the previous three games had started: in control. We went up 14–0 after two touchdown passes to

Plaxico of forty-two and twenty-eight yards, respectively, in the first quarter. We led 17–10 at halftime and were in prime position to win our eighth game in a row. We even led 23–10 at the end of the third quarter. All of a sudden, however, it was like I was back in the year 2000 at Three Rivers Stadium—the second half was riddled with interceptions.

I didn't think too much of it, however. It was a bad game. I had a bad performance. It happens.

We lost, but we were 12–3 and had won the AFC Central Division. We had home field advantage throughout the playoffs.

Later that week, following the loss to the Bengals, I remember sitting in the Steelers cafeteria next to General Manager Kevin Colbert when Coach Cowher approached me.

As I mentioned before, Coach Cowher and I hadn't said much to one another that entire season. In a rare moment, however, he looked at me and asked, "You're human now, huh?"

Maybe he was just trying to be friendly or humorous—I don't know. But it was an interesting moment that, in my mind, perfectly represents how he acted toward me when I was the Steelers' starting quarterback. He didn't say much to me during our seven-game winning streak. But he didn't hesitate to acknowledge my flaws—highlight them, even.

I understood where he might have been coming from—after all, that entire season I was playing out-of-mind, out-of-sight football and I was coming off a game in which I had thrown four interceptions—but I didn't feel like it was the time to say something like that. Sarcastic remarks like that are better left unsaid. It was as if he was saying, "Now you're back to normal, huh?"

Maybe I misinterpreted some of Coach Cowher's intentions or conversations—it's a possibility—but he always seemed to have his doubts about me, and that affected the way I interpreted him during my time at Pittsburgh.

We completed our best season since 1978 with a 28–7 victory against the Cleveland Browns at Heinz Field. It was a celebratory day. Coach Cowher even got caught on camera dancing in the locker room—one of the more interesting sights I've seen.

Though we were 13–3, our record didn't matter one bit.

The playoffs were next, and we, like everyone else, were 0–0.

✦ ✦ ✦

Team owner Dan Rooney told the media that he believed we could win it all. Of all the teams he had seen, in all the years he had been around Pittsburgh Steelers football, he said that this team had something about it that was comparable to past Super Bowl champions he had seen.

"Sure, we can win it all," he told the media. "Definitely, we can."

Oh yeah, Super Bowl XXXVI was also in New Orleans.

My hometown.

✦ ✦ ✦

Baltimore (the No. 5 seed) crushed Miami (the No. 4 seed) 20–3 in the first round of the playoffs, and Oakland (the No. 3 seed) beat the New York Jets (the No. 6 seed) 38–24. Thanks to our 13–3 record, we were the No. 1 seed. New England was the No. 2 seed with an 11–5 record.

This meant that after our first-round bye, we would play Baltimore, which was all too fitting. The team we despised more than any other.

As you may remember, we split the regular season series with Baltimore. They beat us at Heinz Field 13–10 in our seventh game of the year, and we beat them 26–21 at their place in our thirteenth game of the year. Our only loss at Heinz Field that season was to the Baltimore Ravens. We used that as fuel.

We knew we could beat Baltimore. It was just a matter of doing it. Baltimore played with emotion and passion, but when their emotion deflated, they had nothing to rely on. They would talk themselves into thinking they could beat us, so our goal was to strike early and bring them back to reality.

Entering the game, we were also excited for our primary weapon, Jerome Bettis, to make his return. He was feeling good, and he was ready. It felt like everything was lining up properly. We were already winning in his absence, but with him, everything was *really* locked and loaded within our offense.

During warm-ups, however, Jerome felt a "twinge" in his leg, and he went to the locker room to get a shot of painkillers from our team doctor. When he returned to the field, he felt his entire leg going numb, so he returned to the locker room. Apparently, the medication had struck his femoral nerve, thus causing his whole leg to go numb for the next eight hours. Considering he could hardly walk without falling, there wasn't a chance he could play.

It was very difficult news to hear, but Coach Cowher delivered an inspirational pregame speech and prepared us to take the field.

Our defense set the tone from the start, intercepting one of quarterback Elvis Grbac's throws on the opening drive. We connected on a couple of throws on offense and quickly got on the board with a field goal. We scored a touchdown midway through the first quarter to take a 10–0 lead. In the second quarter, we got another touchdown and a field goal to take a 20–0 lead. We were doing exactly what we needed to do: knock them down early.

Speaking of knocking them down early, one funny story from that game is that Hines Ward seemed to get in cornerback Rod Woodson's head right from the start. I liked Rod, and he had even been my teammate in 1995 and 1996, but boy was it fun to watch him and Hines go at it. First off, Hines was a termite—an instigator—and he proudly and deviously loved to eat away at his opponents' mentality until their foundation completely collapsed. To this day, he's a prankster. Most recently, we were at Warrick Dunn's charity golf tournament, and he snuck up behind me and yelled, "BOOM!" He scared the crap out of me. "Man, I'm too old to be scared like that," I said. "Aren't we too big for this?" Hines just chuckled. It's always that same goofy chuckle. *Hehehe, hehehe.* I swear the jokester came out of the womb laughing.

Anyway, by the end of the game I was convinced that Rod wanted to fight Hines with everything within him and at the same time didn't want to fight Hines. The whole Baltimore defense wanted to fight Hines. Hines had been ruthless and relentless, and he had been knocking people's faces off (and maybe sneaking in a few cheap shots) the entirety of the game.

No one fought him, however, and we went on to win 27–10 in front of our home crowd. The game was never even a contest.

We were one step closer.

◆ ◆ ◆

It was satisfying to know we were going back to a big game. The last time I had played in the AFC Championship was against the Denver Broncos in 1997, before all the musical chairs had begun. Having lost that game and having watched the Broncos go on to win the Super Bowl, there were many of us, including myself, who were looking for redemption.

My family and friends were excited, too. My father and his friend, my brother and his wife, my agent Leigh Steinberg, and some of my best friends all came to Pittsburgh for the game. There was nothing I wanted more than to go to the Super Bowl in my hometown of New Orleans. I wanted it with every fiber of my being. All the magic we had made that season culminated in this particular moment. Against New England. At Heinz Field. With our star running back returning to the lineup.

During the first quarter, we went back-and-forth, back-and-forth with the scoreboard stuck at zero, until New England scored on a punt return to take a 7–0 lead at the end of the first.

Kris hit a thirty-yarder in the second quarter to make the score 7–3, and the rest of the second quarter followed the first quarter's back-and-forth trend. New England finally scored near the end of the second, making the score 14–3 and only leaving us a minute to get down the field and cut our deficit before halftime.

We failed to do so; both our running and passing game was struggling. I threw an interception at the end of the half, and we trailed 14–3 in the locker room.

Everything about that game had felt out-of-sync. We had no running game. I do not know how to explain it, but it was as if the Patriots had us figured out, like they knew exactly what we were going to do each play. My agent, Leigh, says that Belichick's game plan that day involved one of the most smothering defenses he had ever seen.

Our special teams continued to struggle in the second half.

New England blocked a field goal attempt at the beginning of the third quarter and ran it back for a touchdown to take a commanding 21–3 lead, which was very deflating. All of a sudden, we were down by eighteen. Our season seemed to flash before our eyes.

Nothing was working smoothly. We had no flow. No momentum. It didn't feel like *us*. It didn't feel at all like the season had felt.

In the third quarter, we finally we went to work.

Eleven-yard pass to Jerome. Twenty-four-yard pass to Hines. Nineteen-yard pass to Amos Zereoue. Nine-yard toss to Hines. Amos for three yards. Jerome up the middle for a yard.

Touchdown.

21–10, New England.

The Patriots went three-and-out, and we took over in New England territory.

Nine-yard pass to Dan Kreider. Ten-yard pass to Plaxico. Amos up the middle for eleven yards.

Touchdown.

21–17, New England.

Heinz Field was roaring.

In the third quarter, we responded like we had responded all season. Relentlessly. Like we were *supposed* to win.

The fourth quarter, however, felt like the first half. We were once again unable to do anything. Adam Vinatieri hit a forty-four-yard field goal for New England at the start of the quarter to make the score 24–17; we punted; they punted; I threw an interception; they missed a field goal; I threw another interception . . . and that was the game and the season. With the exception of a couple of drives in the third quarter, New England completely disrupted our game plan and offense.

Another loss in an AFC Championship game at home. Just like 1997.

Considering the progress we had made that season following our three-year drought, we had every reason to feel good about the season. But it hurt to get that close and fall short. I remember my teammate Wayne Gandy saying that it felt better to go 3–13 when he played for the Saint Louis Rams than to go 13–3 with the Steelers and lose in the AFC Championship.

After the game, Coach Cowher came up to me, patted me on the back, and said, "Don't worry about it, kid. You're still my guy."

✦ ✦ ✦

I went to the Pro Bowl that year for the first time in my career and finished third overall in MVP voting for the league. I was also named the Steelers MVP for the first time in my career.

While in Hawaii for the Pro Bowl, all I could think about was 2002. I wanted to recapture 2001 and get us back to the same spot the following season. I wanted to set things right and get to the Super Bowl, like I knew we could. The 2001 season was great. The Pro Bowl was great. But it wasn't enough. It hurt to think about how close we had gotten.

The 2001 season was a step in the right direction though. Our playoff drought was over. We achieved a number of things that year that many never expected. On a personal note, I was the quarterback again, and people had faith in me again. After the previous three seasons, I felt like I'd jumped straight to the top and skipped all the developmental stages in between.

More than anything, 2001 was a big step in the right direction in regard to our style of play. It felt like we had reverted back to doing things "the Pittsburgh way," and it worked. I couldn't wait to continue building on our success.

22

THE TRANSITION

The offseason was just as interesting and revealing.

The Steelers signed most of their star players—except for me, that is—to long-term contracts.

I had two years left on my contract but wanted to renegotiate. I was hoping to get my contract extended—to be the Steelers' quarterback for another several years. I felt like I had proved my worth in 2001.

Leigh and I went in, and I told them I wanted to renegotiate. "If you like me, then let me stay for a long time," I told Steelers management. "Lock me in. If you like me, lock me in."

They wanted me to simply restructure my contract. I told them I wanted to renegotiate. I wanted to stay in Pittsburgh. After all the fun I had in 2001—are you kidding me? As challenging as 1998, 1999, and 2000 had been, it would all have been worthwhile if it had paved a way for me to have a long, successful career with the Steelers as their starting quarterback for many more seasons. I just felt like it was time. I guess they wanted to see me have another season like 2001 in 2002. They wanted to see if I could do it again. I understood.

In all reality, it presented a great opportunity to have another year like 2001 and then sign an even better contract the next season. That's how I looked at it. The Steelers were taking a risk. If I played poorly, they wouldn't be locked into anything. But if I played well again, my value would rise even more.

I was ready to play well again.

Something I found a little strange, though, was that they made moves with two other quarterbacks that offseason. They resigned backup Tommy Maddox and restructured his contract, and they also signed Charlie Batch, a backup from the Detroit Lions.

✦ ✦ ✦

Throughout the entirety of the offseason, there was a bitter taste in all of our mouths from our AFC Championship defeat against the Patriots. When we found out we would be playing New England the first game of the season, there was a massive build-up to the game. It was our chance to seize our revenge—on national television on Monday night—after being humiliated the year before.

There would be no revenge, however. We lost 30–14 at the brand-new Gillette Stadium to the defending Super Bowl champions. I had two interceptions that day, and, though I didn't realize it at the time, my agent says that game was my death knell in Pittsburgh.

There is no other explanation for what happened next.

✦ ✦ ✦

We lost our second game of the season, too—a 30–17 defeat at Heinz Field against the Oakland Raiders. I think that losing to the Patriots in the playoffs the year before and dropping the first two games of the 2002 season really worked against me.

Luckily, we had a much-needed bye week in Week 3 to regroup and recuperate. That Thursday before we went on vacation, Coach Cowher pulled me into his office. "How ya doing, kid?" he asked me.

"I'm doing pretty good, Coach," I said. "How you doing?"

"I'm doing good," he said, and then paused for a moment. "Ya know," he went on, "you ever watch baseball, and when the starting pitcher isn't doing well, the relief pitcher comes in?"

"Yeah," I said. "As a matter of fact, I played pitcher growing up."

"Well, " he said, "I was thinking about your position and giving you someone who could be a relief pitcher for you at quarterback."

What are you talking about? I thought to myself. It sounded like musical chairs all over again. He was making a statement, but he was saying it very indirectly.

I didn't say anything else—I was processing it all.

Coach Cowher was always looking for a fix. He had let me do my thing the year before, and I think it turned out okay. We ended the season with the most victories in Steelers history since 1978.

It seemed like he was subtly saying, "If you make a mistake, then you are going to get benched." Back to that short leash again. Back to musical chairs again.

When Coach Cowher told me about his "relief pitcher" idea, I felt like the writing was on the wall. Being asked to restructure. Resigning Tommy Maddox. Signing Charlie Batch. It was as if the back-to-back emotional losses to New England the losses in our first two games of 2002 were a perfect excuse to make a change. What better time to do it?

Kordell Stewart, the starter.

Tommy Maddox, his "relief pitcher".

Our Week 3 game against Cleveland was a grind. We trailed 3–0 at the end of the first quarter, entered halftime with the game tied 6–6, and started the fourth quarter with the same score. We were desperate for a win. We couldn't start the season 0–3 like two years before when Kent Graham had been starting. After all, we had only lost three games *total* in 2001.

I was having an average game. No interceptions. More than one hundred yards passing over three quarters. Thirty-some yards in rushing. I was trying to do all I could. We just struggled to get into the end zone.

At the start of the fourth, we were finally marching down the field with a chance to take the lead. We ventured into Cleveland territory, and I completed a seventeen-yard pass to Hines and then a six-yard pass to Plaxico. We were on the Cleveland twenty-eight.

On the next play, I finally threw one toward the end zone—up the middle to Plaxico—but it was picked off in the end zone by Robert Griffith.

I hung my head. "Dammit," I said.

For our next drive, Coach Cowher told me to stay on the bench as he tried out his new "relief pitcher" game plan. I stood by the bench, listening as the fans went crazy over Tommy. Heinz Field got loud, the loudest it had been the entire game.

✦ ✦ ✦

Tommy scored a touchdown on his first drive. Just like that, the solution had been found. Cleveland scored too, and the game went into overtime with the score tied 13–13. Our kicker, Todd Peterson, ultimately hit a thirty-one yarder to win the game.

Tommy did well in that game, especially with all the pressure. I was happy for him. After we won, he was elated, and I went up to him and gave him a high-five. I was excited, too. I was proud of him. It was his time. His moment. And he seized it. But I also wondered: who would be the relief pitcher now? Tommy? Or me?

After the game, Jerome approached me.

"Phew!" he said, hitting me in the chest, overjoyed we had squeezed out a win. "You know," he said, giving it to me straight, "if you would've stayed out there, we still would've won. I know we would have."

I shrugged.

"But it had to happen," I said.

History repeats itself.

◆ ◆ ◆

Though we lost the next game against New Orleans, Tommy gave Coach Cowher something he hadn't seen in a while: an exuberant passing game. He would sometimes throw the ball thirty-five or forty times in a game, which I think Coach found to be a breath of fresh air.

Ever since Tommy had come in after my interception against Cleveland and scored a touchdown, in Cowher's mind, he was *the answer*. Jerome communicates this theory in his book about Coach Cowher benching me for Tommy Maddox:

> *I can't prove it, but in my heart I really believe that Kordell was set up for failure that season. You've got a guy who just took you to the AFC Championship, had one of his best years ever . . . and you're going to give him the quick hook three games into the season? You bench your Pro Bowl quarterback for a guy who had been out of football for years, who hadn't started an NFL game in ten seasons? That just doesn't happen by accident.*

I think they pulled Kordell partly because they didn't want to pay him a big salary and signing bonus. It was cheaper for them if he didn't have success . . . .

We won the next four games, and Tommy started all of them. It was fun to watch, really—he was indeed dynamic in the air. It wasn't *easy* to watch—it felt like I had been forgotten, as if the year before had never happened—but it was fun. Tommy "Guns" Maddox played well.

Tommy and I had a great relationship, and just like I had tried to support Mike Tomczak and Kent Graham, I also tried to support Tommy. That was the position I was in. It was Tommy's team—that's what Coach Cowher had decided—and I could either be bitter about it or try to make Tommy better. How Coach Cowher chose to use me was up to him. I would do my best at playing the role he gave me. Whatever it was.

✦ ✦ ✦

In Week 10 against the Atlanta Falcons, Tommy passed for a franchise-record 473 yards, but the game ended in an unusual 34–34 tie. As good as Tommy was, Michael Vick also had one of the best clutch performances of his career, rallying the Falcons from seventeen points down in the fourth quarter.

In practice heading into the game, I remember Coach Cowher calling Vick's style of play "backyard football." He seemed really fed up with the mobile quarterback. I found this interesting.

In the fourth quarter of that game, as Vick was running the ball all over the place and throwing the ball all over the place, I looked at one of my teammates and said, "Backyard football, huh?"

✦ ✦ ✦

The next week against Tennessee at the Coliseum, Tommy was starting his seventh game in a row, continuing his dominance, and perfecting our passing game.

In the final play of the third quarter, however, Tommy completed a two-yard pass to Antwaan Randle El but took a hard hit and got a concussion on the play, sidelining him for the remainder of the game.

Tennessee ate up a good chunk of time at the start of the fourth quarter and kicked a field goal to take a 31–7 lead with eight minutes to play.

I knew a comeback was unlikely, but I just wanted to go in and do my job.

Before I took the field, I was standing next to linebacker Jason Gildon on the sideline.

"It's your time," he said to me.

From past conversations with Jason, I knew that while he was in college at Oklahoma State University, he had to memorize Edgar Albert Guest's poem, *See It Through*.

"You know that poem 'See It Through'?" I said.

"Yeah, man, you know it, too?" he asked.

"Of course," I said, and I proceeded to recite the entire poem to him.

When you're up against a trouble,
Meet it squarely, face to face;
Lift your chin and set your shoulders,
Plant your feet and take a brace.
When it's vain to try to dodge it,
Do the best that you can do;
You may fail, but you may conquer,
See it through!

Black may be the clouds about you
And your future may seem grim,
But don't let your nerve desert you;
Keep yourself in fighting trim.
If the worst is bound to happen,
Spite of all that you can do,
Running from it will not save you,
See it through!

Even hope may seem but futile,
When with troubles you're beset,

But remember you are facing
Just what other men have met.
You may fail, but fall still fighting;
Don't give up, whate'er you do;
Eyes front, head high to the finish.
See it through!

"Wow," Jason said. "I ain't worried about you. You're good to go, bro."

✦ ✦ ✦

Our entire first drive, Coach Cowher didn't even wear his headset. He didn't need to.

Five-yard pass to Antwaan. Seven-yard pass to Plaxico. Seven-yard pass to Antwaan. Three in a row. Then an incomplete pass.

Ten-yard pass to Hines. Twelve-yard run by Amos Zereoue. Twelve-yard pass to Terance Mathis. Eleven-yard quarterback draw up the middle. Three-yard pass to Antwaan. Three more in a row. One-yard run. Incomplete pass.

Four-yard pass to Terance.

Touchdown.

"That's one," I said to myself.

Pass to Dan Kreider for the two-point conversion.

Good.

31–15.

Tennessee went three-and-out, and we once again took the field. Coach Cowher put his headset back on for this possession.

Eleven-yard pass to Amos. Fourteen-yard pass to Hines. Nine-yard pass to Antwaan. Eleven-yard pass to Amos. Four in a row. Incomplete pass.

Twenty-seven-yard pass to Hines. Incomplete pass. Four-yard pass to Hines.

Touchdown.

"That's two," I said to myself.

Pass to Hines from Antwaan for the two-point conversion.

Good.

31–23.

When I got to the sideline, I went and sat down alone on the bench. Jerome and running back Chris Fuamatu-Ma'afala were on the opposite side of the bench.

"Look, Jerome," Chris said in his Hawaiian accent, "Stew on fi-ah [fire]. He possessed."

I looked at Jerome, and he winked at me.

✦ ✦ ✦

We had a chance to make history that day, but we couldn't recover the onside kick, and the Titans ran out the clock.

Tennessee drained seven minutes from the clock at the start of the quarter, and it killed us. If I had had more time, we would have done it. I know it.

✦ ✦ ✦

Tommy was still injured when we played Cincinnati at Heinz Field the next week, and we picked up right where we'd left off the game before.

We scored on our first drive, pretty much running the Bengals into the ground with Jerome. On our next drive, we scored again. This time, it only took three plays, including a fifteen-yard pass to Jerome and a sixty-four-yard pass to Hines.

As much as I supported Tommy, I wanted to remind everyone that I hadn't gone anywhere. Nor was I going anywhere. I'd be back. I'd always be back. I had proved that the game before. I had proved that the season before. I'd do it again.

The score was close toward the end, but we went on a couple of big drives to secure the win 29–21. I had 236 yards passing, completed twenty-two of twenty-six passes, and had forty yards rushing. It felt like 2001 again.

I never asked 2001 to leave.

They did.

✦ ✦ ✦

We were at a crucial point in our season. Standing at 6¬–4–1 and fighting for a playoff spot, our victory against Cincinnati had been a big one as we flirted with falling to .500 on the year. Our game the upcoming week against Jacksonville would be just as important.

I had the same confidence and carries the same chip on my shoulder, and we won 25–23. Again.

We had gone 2–0 when I started in place of Tommy, and we nearly pulled off a miracle win in the game where he went down.

✦ ✦ ✦

The following week against the Texans, Tommy returned and started. At one point during the game, after Tommy had thrown a couple of interceptions, I remember Coach Cowher yelling to him, "What did we talk about?"

I have no idea what Coach Cowher meant, but I felt as if him and Tommy had their own little thing going on. Because I was emotionless by this point, I saw things I wouldn't have normally have seen. I think Coach Cowher knew that if Tommy messed up, then he'd be forced to start me.

Again, I knew the writing was on the wall. I said to myself, *I'm going to accept it for what it is, and let whatever happens happen.* I had reached the end of my rope trying to prove a point, and nothing was a surprise anymore. I was numb to it all.

Coach Clements talked to Tommy and me following his interception, as he always did with the quarterbacks following a possession. Then I went to the cooler, got a drink of Gatorade, and walked toward the other end of the bench. I sat down, and it felt like I had an outer-body experience. I know that's not what it was, but I saw everything happening slowly and vividly on the sideline in front of me. Unlike the year before, I saw Coach Cowher being *very* involved. He was talking with Coach Clements, and his demeanor appeared very hands-on and desperate. It seemed like he really wanted the offense with Tommy at the helm to be a success.

Stay in your lane, I said to myself. *Stay physically in it, stay mentally in it, and be prepared. It's not your battle anymore.*

We might have lost that day to the Texans, but I would never start for the Steelers again.

23

'THANKS FOR HELPING US'

"Hey, kid," Coach Cowher said, getting my attention as we crossed paths in the Steelers practice facility.

I turned around.

"How ya doing?" he asked.

"I'm doing good," I answered.

"Well, just wanted to tell ya somethin'," he continued. "Thanks for helping us."

The way he said it was dismissive, like my time was done. He said "us"—as in the team—like he was talking about himself and all the other players but not me. Like I wasn't part of the team. Like I was disaster relief that comes in and is quickly forgotten once everything goes back to normal. I guess the "relief pitcher" theory did work. We went 2–0.

Thanks for helping us.

I didn't say anything. It was my job as a player to respect Coach Cowher and the decisions he made. He knew what he meant. I knew what he meant. We both knew. Time seemed to stop. I just looked at him.

I finally opened my mouth.

"Whatever you need, Coach," I said. "Whenever you need me again, I'm here."

At that moment, I knew my days in Pittsburgh were over. And it felt like the weight of the world had been lifted off my shoulders.

✦ ✦ ✦

I say that the "weight of the world had been lifted off my shoulders," because in that moment, I realized how exhausting playing for the Steelers had been—especially that season. As sad an ending as it was, I felt peace that I no longer had to deal with the things I had been dealing with for so long.

I walked into our team meeting feeling proud, feeling good about myself, feeling that I had accomplished everything I possibly could in 2001 and even 2002. Tommy got hurt. I came in. I got the job done. I detached myself emotionally from the Pittsburgh Steelers, because I knew right then and there that it was the end.

Sitting in that meeting, I was emotionless, to be honest. In one sense, I took this latest slight very personally. I took a lot of things that happened in Pittsburgh personally. But at the same time, those seven years only made me work harder. The adversity didn't break me. It didn't do anything but make me stronger. It just made me play for it; it made me dissect film; it made me work a little bit harder; it made me that much more determined.

Remember the movie *Blade*? In Pittsburgh, I tried to *use* the frustrations to my advantage. I *used* the lies said about me to strengthen my willpower and determination to prove a point on the football field. I *used* it to fuel my desire to get it done. No matter what position you're in or what circumstances you face, grind on, grind on, grind on. That's all you can do. Everything else is beyond your control. Says Jerome Bettis in his book, which was released in 2007:

> With Kordell, you always ask yourself, "What if?" What if there had been a long-term commitment made to him by the coaching staff? What if he hadn't played wide receiver his rookie year and instead had concentrated on learning how to be an NFL quarterback? What if they had found an offensive coordinator who could have designed an offense to benefit Kordell?....
>
> And still, he was good enough to get us to the playoffs and to two AFC Championships. He was good enough to go 46–30 as a starter. Only Terry Bradshaw has thrown for more yards as a Steeler. And Kordell is still the thirteenth-leading rusher in team history.

Through it all, I took peace in this: I gave everything I possibly could. Through the different offensive coordinators, the musical chairs with quarterbacks, the rumors, and the personal attacks, I gave everything.

I may not have had the best stats in Pittsburgh. I may not have been appreciated the most in Pittsburgh. I may not have felt like things were necessarily fair in Pittsburgh. But I left that city a winner. My record stands for itself. I left Pittsburgh a winner. Period. No more. No less.

So I'm hanging my hat on being a winner in that city. How many quarterbacks can say that they went to two AFC Championships in the two years when they started every game?

When I was given the opportunity, I got it done.

And I appreciated the opportunity. That's the mindset I kept coming back to. Whereas there was definitely some conflict in Pittsburgh, I appreciated Coach Cowher giving me the chance to do everything I had always dreamed of doing as a professional on the football field.

My *experiences* in Pittsburgh—every one of them—made me better.

The positive things reminded me to thank God for His kindness. The negative things became *lessons* that made me a better person for God. How can you lose? My testimony is through my experiences, not through my words (though I appreciate your reading these words), and it's for anyone who wants to learn from it or follow it.

No matter has happened or will happen in my life, I have the mindset that I am always *gaining*. I am always *winning*.

Pittsburgh was tough, but it showed me that I could dig deeper than I thought I could on my own. The emotional feeling of getting up day after day and pressing on and seeing it through allowed me to dig deeper than I ever imagined.

That's one of the many reasons why I loved Pittsburgh and still do.

PART III

FATHER

24

A SON OF MY OWN

Following the 2002 season, the Steelers cut ties with me, as I had expected might happen, and I was picked up by the Chicago Bears.

I had always loved Chicago. It was great to go to another legendary organization—a historical organization with a historical stadium, Soldier Field. On top of that, the stadium was newly renovated, so it was a cool experience to be a part of the team at that time, just as it had been neat to be on the Steelers when Heinz Field was introduced.

Chicago is, hands down, one of the best cities in the country. It became one of my favorite cities while living there. Michigan Avenue is one of the cleanest, nicest places to visit (and live). I had a downtown condominium, next to Tavern on Rush and Gold Coast and a big church cathedral, and I enjoyed having the opportunity to live in one of my favorite cities and experience all its festivities firsthand—how they dyed the Chicago River green on St. Patrick's Day and hosted the Taste of Chicago (one of the largest food festivals in the world) every summer.

The biggest news for me following my time in Pittsburgh, however, came on a personal level.

In May 2003, before my season with the Bears, my longtime girlfriend, Tania, gave birth to my first and only child—a baby boy whom we named Syre. To respect the privacy of those involved in my past relationships, I have refrained from talking about them throughout the duration of this book. I will say, however, that my relationship with Tania was the most serious relationship I'd had up to that point; at one point, we were even engaged. We had several conversations about kids, and we ended up having one.

Though many athletes aren't so fortunate, I was blessed to be in

Philadelphia, where Tania lived at the time, for my son's birth. She lived there because that was where her mom lived; this helped give her some support while I was playing football. I hated that it had to be that way, but it was the best thing for her (and for us) while I was playing football. I wouldn't have missed his birth for the world. Words cannot explain what I saw that day. I was scared to hold Syre initially because he was so fragile. All I wanted to do was wrap him up in blankets and talk to him as he lay in the hospital crib under a light. Holding him was terrifying.

We decided to name him Syre because of Run-D.M.C.'s lyrics ("I'm the king of rock. There is none higher. Sucka MCs should call me sire") in their song "King of Rock". My son is awesome! Just look at his name!

I knew that Syre's birth would change my life forever. In a sense, I felt like all my life experiences climaxed at that moment in a hospital room in Philadelphia. Everything I had experienced—the loss in my family and the challenges in Pittsburgh, the people who came into my life along the way, the strangers I met, the coaches who helped me, the little things my brother did when I was a kid, the ways my mom and sister lived and loved, the way my cousins were, the way my aunts and uncles cared for me, the ministers at the church who were instrumental in our lives—everything led up to this moment of becoming a father. It all fed into the maturation process so I felt ready and prepared to have a kid of my own. The story is written before you live it—it's about understanding what the story is. Looking at my newborn son that day in the hospital, I had a better understanding of what that story was.

✦ ✦ ✦

When the NFL season began once more, Tania usually looked after Syre in Philadelphia during the week, and then they travelled to Chicago to be with me over the weekends. Syre's first flight was when he was three weeks old. Despite the inconsistent lifestyle of being a professional athlete, we wanted to make sure Syre had a father figure in his life from the get-go.

Once that winter, I remember walking down Michigan Avenue with Tania and Syre to go shopping. We wanted to find Syre one of those big, furry bodysuits because it was so cold in the city. At one point, we came around a corner, and the chilling wind whipped down the street and hit us all right in the face. Syre, who was probably only six months old at the time, started making a noise from the back of his throat. The wind was so strong that he was struggling to breathe. I picked him up and cradled him to my chest. He slobbered all over his daddy. It was really quite funny, not to mention adorable. As they say in the South where I was raised, I just wanted to eat him up.

Professionally, I started about seven games under head coach Dick Jauron, who I really liked, and we finished with a 7–9 record. Overall, it was kind of a lackluster year, despite improving from the Bears' 4–12 record the previous year.

All this is to say, my best memories that year weren't on the football field. Rather, they came while spending time with my family. Tania, Syre, and I made some great memories together that year in Chicago. Tania videotaped many of these memories, and just recently, when Syre was eleven years old, we watched the tapes with him at Christmas. He had never seen video footage from that time in his life, and he was so moved that he actually started crying.

"Love you, Dad," he told me.

"I love you, Son," I said.

25

END OF FOOTBALL, BEGINNING OF LIFE

After one year with the Bears, I was picked up by the Steelers' archrival, the Baltimore Ravens. It was weird at first to give myself over to the rival, but I was grateful to be on their team. Though we had some big-time battles during my days with the Steelers, I had tons of respect for them. They had even won a Super Bowl in 2000.

Over those next two seasons, 2004 and 005, I only played three games as a backup quarterback. I could tell I was in the final stretch of my career. After being the starting quarterback on a team that went to the AFC Championship in 2001, I would never experience the same success in the NFL again—my career never rose to the point that it had in Pittsburgh.

When Pittsburgh eventually won the Super Bowl in 2005 with quarterback Ben Roethlisberger at the helm, I called Coach Cowher after their victory and told him, "Congratulations, Coach."

"Thank you, man," he said to me. "You know, I wasn't expecting this."

"Well, you deserve it, Coach," I said.

"Yeah, thank you, Slash," he said genuinely. "You know, the crazy thing is that we had to bring Ben [Roethlisberger] along sort of the same way we brought you along. He's a mirror image of how you played the game. You ran around. You made plays. He's just a little bit bigger than you in size. Those were some good times," he reflected. "Some tough times, but some good times."

✦ ✦ ✦

I don't think I was as connected with my teammates in Chicago or Baltimore, because football was truly a job at this point. With the Steelers, it was a lifestyle. But now I had a family. They were my primary concern. The moment Syre was born, he became the most important thing in my life. Nothing else seemed to matter quite as much.

While I was with the Ravens, Tania and Syre often drove from Philadelphia to Baltimore to see me or flew to watch my games on the road. Because of how frequently Syre flew, I noticed during those toddler years that he *loved* airplanes. Because of this, I used to hold him with his chest parallel to the ground and "fly" him around the house. He always kicked his feet like he was going somewhere, like he was swimming or something. He'd slobber everywhere, just kicking his little butt off. Whenever he saw an airplane, he'd always say, "Air-pane! Air-pane! Air-pane! Huuuuuuuuuge!"

As I moved on from the NFL after my 2005 season with the Ravens, I was able to spend even more time with him. I tried to raise him to the best of my ability and was often reminded of how my parents had raised me—how they spent quality time with Robert, Falisha, and me throughout our lives, and how, when Momma passed, Daddy took me everywhere with him while he worked at his jobsites around New Orleans.

In 2008, Tania and I decided to call off our engagement and go our separate ways. Although we didn't end up working out, she was an amazing mother to Syre and continues to be an amazing mother to him. Much like my own parents, Tania and I did not allow our own relationship and its struggles to affect our relationships with our son. We still have a very good relationship between us.

Upon our split, however, we had to make decisions about how we would take care of Syre. Unlike many fathers today, I really wanted to be a part of my son's life on a consistent, daily basis—similar to how my father had been a part of my life growing up. As I said before, I saw it as my duty as a man to take care of my son. Tania and I came to an agreement, and she trusted me to take primary care of him.

Sometimes a mother doesn't know what might happen if Daddy gets the kids, but Tania trusts me enough to spend most of the year with Syre. (He spends summers with her in Los Angeles.) I don't go out to the clubs or strip clubs—never have, never will. I'm a social kind of person. I'll have a social drink or a social dinner. Sometimes I'll go out and listen to good music—socially. But I'm not interested in partying, nor am I interested in being "seen by people" or trying to "stay relevant." I don't care about all that. I care about those who are closest to me. I care about my son. No matter what opportunities or situations might come my way in my post-NFL career, I'm committed to keeping Syre as my No. 1 concern. There is nothing more fulfilling and meaningful to me than being a father.

The key to life is knowing that someone is there for you, and I always want Syre to know I'm there for him—not just physically, but also emotionally, spiritually, and mentally. I understood how important it is to simply *be there*—because a parent's presence, or lack of presence, has an effect over time. As a man, it was my *duty* to be there for him. Not my choice. My duty. It was my duty to be with him, to help him understand how to respect his elders, and to help him become a man—because one day, my time would be up, too. I love my son, and I have never regretted making my parenting of him the most important aspect of my life.

26

THE BEST MAN I EVER KNEW

Just as I enjoyed spending more time with my own son in my post-NFL life, one of the things I enjoyed most about being done with football was having more time to spend with my father. With football over, there was no timeline and no restrictions, so we started traveling a lot more. I still tried to stay in shape, just in case football reentered the picture, and I kept plenty busy—working as an analyst at ESPN for four years along with being a sideline reporter for the short-lived and now defunct United Football League (UFL)—but I still had more time and flexibility to travel with my dad and be with family.

Playing golf became one of my and Dad's favorite things to do together. He was an active man, but also a man advancing in age. Golf was a perfect fit. A couple times, I took him to Pebble Beach Golf Links on the coast of California. He *loved* Pebble Beach, and it was awesome to experience it with him. We also played at a golf course I belonged to in Pinehurst, North Carolina. We spent weekends and sometimes entire weeks together in North Carolina, playing golf together every day and hanging out with one another.

Of course, he also loved spending time with Syre. Though I was the youngest of three siblings, Syre was my father's first biological grandchild.

Getting Dad a Super Bowl ticket or taking him to Pebble Beach might have been neat, but giving him his first grandchild was priceless.

✦ ✦ ✦

I think a story that encapsulates the way my father viewed the world is when he was in the hospital in 2011 with Stage 4 pancreatic cancer. He was in a weak state—the weakest I had ever seen him— and it was apparent to both my brother and I that he was most likely entering his final days of life.

One evening, I was sitting on the sofa in his hospital room when he got out of bed to go to the bathroom. First, however, he walked over to me, leaned over, put his hand on me, and said, "Don't take life too serious, son. Enjoy yourself."

Here was a man whose physical strength was very nearly gone yet who was still trying to be strong for me. That was his outlook, to not take life too seriously—comedy at its best.

"All right," I promised him.

✦ ✦ ✦

No more than two weeks later, my dad passed away at the age of sixty-nine. I went back to Nineveh Baptist Church in Metairie, Louisiana, for the funeral, and we had him buried in a wall next to my mother's and sister's caskets. My brother Terrance's name was on the wall as well. And my three cousins were also buried in the same area.

I remember standing in front of the wall, staring at the names of family members whom I loved—three of my immediate family members, six family members total. All gone. I wasn't even forty years old yet. My father—the person closest to me in all the world—was on the other side of the wall. It was all very weird. What if I was next? What would happen to Syre?

I knew that not having my father and best friend—someone I relied on when I lost my mother, cousins, and sister, someone I talked to constantly amidst all the rumors and scrutiny in Pittsburgh— would be extremely new territory for me. However, as I reflected on my father's life, I was filled with gratitude for the life he lived. Had it not been for him, I would never have been the player I was in the NFL. And most importantly, had it not been for him, I would not be the father that I am today.

27
CLOSURE

2011 was a year of significant transition for me. I lost my best friend, my father, but I gained a new one, my wife, Porsha Williams, as we began a new and exciting life together.

I had never been one to settle down, but Porsha was exactly what I was looking for. She had many qualities I had been praying for, and she seemed to be a godsend. Not only was she beautiful; she also had a great sense of humor, was well respected, and came from a great family. She had accepted her calling as an ordained minister. Her mom, Diane Williams, was an elder. *And* she was the granddaughter of civil rights leader Hosea Williams.

I think it was because of these changes that I decided to officially retire from the NFL in 2012. I understand that might sound strange, considering I hadn't even played in an NFL game since my final season with Baltimore in 2005—nearly seven years before—but there were a number of times over that period of not playing that I toyed with the idea of making a return. I had remained in good shape during that time and believed, as a man in my mid to late thirties, that I still had what it took to play professionally. I was actually put in free agency at one point but wasn't picked up by any team. A return to the NFL might have been a lot of fun, but I also enjoyed the more consistent lifestyle I had of working for the media, spending ample time with my father and my son, and focusing on my family.

In 2012, I decided it was time for closure regarding my football career. I think that losing my father, getting married, and being on the brink of turning forty played into my mindset of finding closure and officially moving on from a sport I loved. In June, I signed a one-day contract with the Steelers and announced my retirement.

I decided to retire as a Steeler because Pittsburgh is where I spent some of the best years of my life.

I loved Pittsburgh and will forever love Pittsburgh. Not only is it a remarkable city; the culture is also impeccable. Pittsburgh is full of generations and generations of families, a bunch of blue-collar people who are hard workers and appreciate the little things. Pittsburgh is a big, little city where everybody knows everybody. The makeup of the people and the passion that runs through the Monongahela River, Allegheny River, and Ohio River is sometimes overwhelming. As an athlete, you have passion; but people from Pittsburgh have passion in general—from the paint shops, to the barbershops, to the grocery stores. Pittsburgh has an intimate, passionate feel to it that is unique to American cities. And boy do those people love their Steelers, Penguins, and Pirates.

When I returned to Pittsburgh to retire, I went to a resort called Nemacolin, about an hour and a half from downtown Pittsburgh. Nemacolin is where Mario Lemieux, the former Pittsburgh Penguins hockey great and current team owner, runs his annual charity event. The golf course is a beautiful Pete Dye design and is owned by Joe Hardy III, the man who founded 84 Lumber. I spent two or three days there, golfing every day. It was the perfect way for me to retire: quietly.

My return was a little awkward, because since my playing days, the Steelers had gone to two Super Bowls with Ben Roethlisberger. Being a quarterback who hadn't won a Super Bowl and going back when they had won—well, I just didn't know how I was going to be received. I'll be honest: walking through the facility for the first time since my departure from the Steelers was very, very weird.

But I was also welcomed with open arms, and I'm thankful for that. I remember shaking hands with their new head coach, Mike Tomlin, who started coaching there in 2007. We're actually about the same age, but he said to me, "Man, good to meet you. I've watched you since I was young." I also sat down and had lunch with Art Rooney II, who is now running the ship for the Steelers. He's a good man, just like his father, Dan Rooney.

The Rooney family took care of me in Pittsburgh. I played in Chicago and Baltimore, but what'd you think I was going to do? Retire as a Chicago Bear? Or as a Baltimore Raven? Heck no. I wanted to be a Steeler for life.

It's true that some things hadn't panned out the way I had hoped in Pittsburgh, but Coach Cowher and the Rooneys gave me an opportunity I'll forever be grateful for. The Steelers gave me some of the most difficult years of my life but also some of the best ones. I'll remember 'em for the best.

28

SEPARATE WAYS

The same year I retired, I got a job as an afternoon radio host at *92.9 The Game*, a CBS radio affiliate in Atlanta. I really liked the job. It was fun being on air on a daily basis, and the people were great. The consistent Monday through Friday schedule was also beneficial for raising a family and being there for Syre and Porsha on a consistent basis.

That same year, *The Real Housewives of Atlanta*, a reality television show on *Bravo*, approached Porsha about being on the show. I admit I was a bit hesitant. I had heard about all the marriages reality television had destroyed, but because Porsha wanted to do it, I went along with it. It was an opportunity for her to achieve some of her professional dreams, and I believed it was my role as her husband to support her in that. Perhaps our relationship could even have an impact on viewers.

As I unlocked the doors and allowed *Bravo*'s camera crews into our house and our lives, however, all the existing problems in our marriage seemed to be brought to light. This is not pleasant to write about, but over time—though I have always believed that divorce should be avoided at all costs—I felt like my only choice was to file for divorce, because the lifestyle was having a negative impact on my young, impressionable son and a detrimental effect on the household I had established. That is all I will say about what transpired.

The show made the divorce process worse, but I chose to keep my mouth shut. Whenever you see people running their mouths about things, it's difficult, especially when those things are not true, but the reality is that I have a child who is more important than a foolish reality television show and people who are trying to make themselves relevant.

At the end of the day, the divorce happened, and I had to move on. My family is ten times better now. This is not a bitter conversation—the divorce was good for everyone. It's one of the hardest things I've ever had to do, but now all parties are better from it. Most importantly, I can be around my son and have the right, positive energy around him.

29

MASTER OF MY FATE

When my mother passed away in my childhood, I was eleven years old. As I have said, her passing drastically changed my relationship with my father. Dad and I became each other's backbone and joy. We did everything together, and, with my sister and brother being a little older, Dad and I spent a lot of time together every day.

Oddly, by the time my and Porsha's divorce was settled in 2014, Syre was also eleven years old. Like my own father, I am currently also a single parent. Though Daddy has passed from this world and into the next, I draw a lot of strength today from the way he raised me back then.

Now, our roles are reversed, and it's almost as if I can feel his presence in how I raise Syre. I miss Daddy—just as I miss Momma, my cousins, and my sister—but now it's as if I can identify with him in a new, profound way, by taking what he did with me and attempting to do the exact same thing with Syre. And then some.

The most valuable lesson my parents taught me—whether it was Momma's attitude as she battled cancer or Daddy's strength in parenting three children on his own—is one I have tried to apply in every phase of my life: to adapt and get it done, and do so while enjoying life and smiling every now and then. I hope I can pass all this down to Syre.

Most in this life will experience all or a variety of these three things: the pain of losing someone, the anguish of unfairness in what is said about you, and the tragedy of heartbreak. Still, we are challenged to have a positive and meaningful response in the midst of negativity. For me, no matter what happened in my life and no matter what happens in my life in the future, I am determined not to let any trial enslave me and push me down a path toward bitterness.

Because of my foundation and the support I received from family and friends throughout my life, my goal was to never deviate from my truth. There are plenty of people who have had a far more difficult life than I have, but I hope my story will still encourage those who read it to view the glass as half-full rather than half-empty.

I have made my own mistakes in this life, and other times I have been on the wrong end of other people's mistakes. But one thing I can control is pressing on instead of dragging my feet, seeing things through instead of allowing my vision to become cloudy, smiling instead of frowning, getting better instead of bitter, viewing the glass as half-full instead of half-empty, and venturing through this life as one who is blessed instead of who is a victim.

As I have learned, this world we live in will inevitably let us down. But the only thing I *can* control is my reaction to the letdowns. The only thing I can control is how I see it through, how I press on toward the finish, and how I adapt—how I adapt as Slash.

————

Invictus

Out of the night that covers me,
Black as the pit from pole to pole,
I thank whatever gods may be
For my unconquerable soul.

In the fell clutch of circumstance
I have not winced nor cried aloud.
Under the bludgeonings of chance
My head is bloody, but unbowed.

Beyond this place of wrath and tears
Looms but the Horror of the shade,
And yet the menace of the years
Finds and shall find me unafraid.

It matters not how strait the gate,
How charged with punishments the scroll,
I am the master of my fate,
I am the captain of my soul.

-William Ernest Henley

————